FROM VIOLENCE TO PEACE

CONFLICT, ETHICS, AND SPIRITUALITY

I

Ramón Martínez de Pisón

From Violence to Peace

Dismantling the Manipulation of Religion

PEETERS
LEUVEN – PARIS – WALPOLE, MA
2013

A catalogue record for this book is available from the Library of Congress.

ISBN 978-90-429-2919-7
D/2013/0602/82

"Blessed are the peacemakers, for they will be called children of God"
(Mt 5:9)

Table of Contents

Acknowledgments

I wish to express my most sincere gratitude to those who helped me bring this research to a successful completion. In the first place, I would like to thank my research assistant, Dr. Lauren M. Levesque. Her aid in preparing an annotated bibliography on religion and violence and her several readings of the manuscript played an essential role in its improvement. In this regard, I express my appreciation to the Research Services and International Services Department of Saint Paul University for the two research grants I received between 2008 and 2011, which enabled me to complete this project.

I owe a special debt of thankfulness to some of my colleagues at Saint Paul University: Professors L. Gregory Bloomquist, Marcel Dumais (emeritus), Eugene King (retired), Robert Michel (retired), Dale M. Schlitt, and Mark Slatter. They read all or some of the text, revised its English expression, and offered very important suggestions concerning the coherence of my argumentation.

In a particular way, I would like to recognize Professor Miriam K. Martin, with whom I have already co-authored a published article and who has always been a source of inspiration for my own research. In Chapters 3, 4 and 6, I draw on some of the reflections from a paper we gave at the International Interdisciplinary Colloquium on the Family, organized by the Sisters of Our Lady of the Cross Chair in Christian Family Studies (Saint Paul University), the "Institut de Pastorale du Collège Universitaire Dominicain de Montréal," and the Faculty of Human Sciences (Saint Paul University), held at Saint Paul University (Ottawa, May 6–8, 2010) on the topic, "The Family's Many Faces." The title of our paper was: "Does Religion Still Condone Violence against Women?: An Application to Women within the Family Context." In this paper we spoke of the consequences of violence for women, and highlighted the patriarchal structures that keep an unfair situation alive. I have modified, and/or reshaped, the content integrated here in order to relate it better to the present study.

In addition, I am indebted to the following persons:

• My confrere, Normand Brûlé, whose pastoral experience with the aboriginal people of James Bay and whose expertise as a professional counselor bring him into direct contact with the suffering of men and women and with the negative consequences of violence in their lives. His comments have deepened my understanding of these issues.

• My family physician and friend, Juan L. Escudero. As a senior health professional, he has been in continuous contact with his patients and seen their physical pain and the psychological suffering. He is well aware of the suffering inflicted upon people in God's name. His sensitivity to religious matters and his knowledge of the three monotheistic religions were indispensible.

• Michael Rock, Professor (retired) of Leadership Studies (Emotional Intelligence), whose help with English expressions in the manuscript has been greatly appreciated.

• Herminio de la Red Vega, OSA, editor of the Spanish journal *Religión y Cultura*, for permission to use, in Chapters 1 and 2, some of the preliminary results of my investigation of the topic, which were previously published in the article "Religión y Violencia" (LVI/253-254 [2010], pp. 479-502).

• The students in my course on Religion and Violence in the Fall of 2011. They were the first with whom I shared what would become the fruits of my research published in this volume. Their questions and comments made an invaluable contribution, for which I am most grateful.

• Dr. J. Harold Ellens, founding editor and editor in chief (1974–1989) of the *Journal of Psychology and Christianity*, for his expert guidance in my publishing endeavors.

Finally, but not least, I would like to pay tribute to my late colleague, Professor J. Kevin Coyle (1943–2010). His generosity and insights helped me enormously to improve the quality of my publications. His advice was particularly important in shaping the Table of Contents of this publication.

Introduction

Following the terrorist attacks on the World Trade Center (New York) and the Pentagon (Virginia) on September 11, 2001, and those perpetrated on four trains in Madrid, Spain, on March 11, 2004, among others, it has become of great urgency to carry out research into the relationship between religion and violence. Until now, most of this research has been carried out in the United States and in Europe. In Canada, we have just begun to study this issue. This is one of the reasons why I have decided to pursue my own research on religion and violence. I focused it on the three monotheistic religions–Judaism, Christianity, and Islam.[1] One of the points that has surprised me most in my initial findings was the apparent lack of "critical thinking" on the part of many people, including religious leaders, politicians, statesmen and women, who failed to thoroughly analyze the problem of religion and violence.

In the first chapter of this more extended study, then, I discuss the various points, in both ancient and contemporary cultures, at which people have moved away from understanding the role of religion as an instrument of social harmony, cultural identity and peace to a consideration of religion as justifying violence. In order to make this shift, communities have embarked on a process of demonizing others–the enemies–and have constructed distorted images of God. This situation has been facilitated by the marriage between religion and the State (Chapter 1).

Furthermore, violence itself has been transformed into a religion which generates destruction and death. Violence carried out in God's name, however, is the most flagrant distortion of the Divine linked to this religion. If, as believers, we should not use God's name as a motivation for violence, then we must also acknowledge the ways in which counter-violence carried out in the name of the same God cannot be morally justified. The line drawn between "terrorism" and "State violence" is thin and fragile (Chapter 2).

The consequences of violence are enormous, long-lasting, and sometimes, permanent. Violence erodes human dignity, destroys community,

[1] To be sure, belonging to the Christian tradition, to the Roman Catholic in particular, I cannot speak on religion and violence within Judaism and Islam with the same accuracy and depth as I do when speaking about Christianity.

and distorts culture. Tragically, violence touches the most vulnerable in society, namely, children, adolescents, aboriginal peoples, the LGBTQ (Lesbian, Gay, Bisexual, Transgender, and Queer) community, and women. Violence also damages the environment (Chapter 3).

With the growing interest in religion and violence, it is a relatively easy matter to examine this relationship from a historical perspective. Many have proposed theories as to why the religious justification of violence still occurs today and give witness to its negative consequences. It is a more difficult matter, however, to understand more specifically why violence is perpetrated in God's name, when Yahweh, the God of Abraham, of Isaac, of Jacob, of Jesus Christ, and of the prophet Muhammad (ca. 570/571–632), is often portrayed as a God of peace, justice, love, mercy, compassion and forgiveness. In order to understand how the three monotheistic religions can give rise to variously developed religious justifications of violence, I have developed five approaches (Chapter 4).

In the first of these approaches, I intend to show how the religious justification of violence is not simply the result of a literal, fundamentalist, and/or selective interpretation of sacred texts of the three monotheistic faiths. More significantly is the fact that their Holy Scriptures, which are considered to have God as their true author, contain toxic texts that justify violence in God's name. Yet, an important point to remember is that texts do not kill by themselves. People are always involved in any religious justification of violence.

In the second approach, I show how religious violence is also the result of patriarchy. I consider patriarchy to be a substratum underlying most of the religious justification of violence. Patriarchy remains powerfully present in religious traditions today, poisoning chances for better gender equality and for the healing of the environment.

In the third approach–and here I present the more important thesis for analyzing the link between religion and violence–I point out the negative role that shame plays in violence. I have dealt with the topic of shame in the past, particularly in its relationship to suicide.[2] Here I address its connection to the religious justification of violence. Shame is a powerful, and for the most part, a very negative emotion, whose consequences have not been taken sufficiently into account until just

[2] See Ramón Martínez de Pisón, *Death by Despair: Shame and Suicide*, New York: Peter Lang Publishing, Inc. (American University Studies. Series VII: Theology and Religion, 245), 2006.

recently. A person who feels ashamed usually evaluates himself or herself in a distorted way and, more particularly, as someone diminished in relationship to oneself, to others, and to God. To feel ashamed is, then, to feel defective globally, and to appear exposed to the possibly painful scrutiny of others. Often, people do not recognize the presence of shame in their lives, even if its consequences in one's life are visible to others. This is the result of what is called "bypassed" shame. Though in a sense, both shame and humiliation are caused, among other factors, by violence, at the same time shame is a powerful trigger for violence. Thus, people can enter into a spiral of violence through feelings of shame and humiliation.

In the fourth approach, I underline the "ideological conception" of globalization, which, especially in its more perverse forms, denies diversity and oppresses the poor. I understand the ideological conception of globalization to refer to the processes through which rich countries impose their neoliberal economic models on poorer countries. This imposition does not respect the unique and diverse cultures of the poorer nations. The result is cultural homogenization.

Finally, in the fifth approach, I discuss the culture of violence, destruction, and death that currently operates in our societies. Violence, in all of its manifestations, has become a form of entertainment and a distraction against boredom. This desensitization to violence can contribute to the justification of violence in God's name by normalizing and legitimizing violence as a way of solving problems.

Taking into consideration these five approaches for understanding the impact of violence, I propose in the next step in my research to re-envision the relationship between religion and culture in order to promote a sustainable peace (Chapter 5). I will do so by highlighting six dimensions, so to speak, of this process of re-envisioning. The first is the "desacralization" of any religious justification of violence. To do so, believers need to develop a hermeneutical interpretation of the Bible and of the Qur'an which questions a literal understanding of God as the true author of these Sacred Books. In spite of such literal, fundamentalist, and/or selective interpretation of Holy Scriptures, which would allow for the divine sanction of violence, a contemporary reading of these Sacred Books should not support any violence carried out in God's name.

The second dimension is gender equality. If patriarchy is at the basis of much of the violence perpetrated in the name of God, past and present, there needs to be greater fostering of gender equality. Indeed, religious communities have become increasingly aware of the relationship between patriarchy, religion and violence, thanks in great part to the efforts of various women's movements.

Taking into account how violence engenders shame and humiliation and the fact that it can become a source of further violence, we come to see that the third dimension is the need to facilitate the empowerment of both individuals and oppressed countries through the healing of shame. To do so, it will be necessary to develop a more just socio-economic, political, environmental and religious order. The healing of personal and social shame is a condition *sine qua non* for overcoming violence.

The fourth dimension to this process of re-envisioning the relationship between religion and culture is the need to develop a "utopian conception" of globalization. A more just conception of globalization can make an important contribution to the advancement of global equality and a rekindling of people's relationship with the environment. Contrary to its "ideological conception," in this model globalization represents the renewal of an old and contemporary dream for international solidarity and ecological justice.

The fifth dimension underlines the necessity of facilitating processes of reconciliation. This requires recalling the violence of the past in order to establish the truth of what really happened. At the same time, this presupposes listening to victims' voices, which are oftentimes silenced by the perpetrators.

Finally, the sixth dimension involves the way in which religion and culture should be re-envisioned exclusively from within a paradigm of peace. This is one of the best ways in which religion can contribute to contemporary public life.

The separation between religion and the State is a relatively new phenomenon. However, contemporary societies are now witnessing a "friendly reconciliation" and, perhaps, a new "courtship" between religion and politics, all the while respecting each their own boundaries. Encouraged by this reconciliation, religion and politics should be conceived as being, together, in service of the human search for peace and a better world (Chapter 6).

I would like to make one important point clear. Despite religion's association with violence in the past, and despite the wrongful use of God's name in the present, the most important criterion for discerning the "authenticity" of any religion today and the "veracity" of its Holy Scriptures, is peace. For this reason, I would like to extend an invitation to all religions and their followers to move away from any tendencies to violence and to become peacemakers. Peace should become the "soul" and the "lungs" of all religions and, thus, the centre of interreligious dialogue. For this reason, I have chosen the passage: "Blessed are the peacemakers, for they will be called children of God" (Mt 5:9) for the overall motif of and guiding inspiration for this study. To become peacemakers is to continue to receive the true message of peace from the God of Abraham. When we listen to this call, we listen to God's word for today's world. Thus, the main purpose for writing this book is to remind believers and religious leaders, particularly those belonging to Judaism, Christianity, and Islam, of the incompatibility between religion and violence.

To conclude, how may we define violence and peace? Provoked violence is an assault on the inviolability of human dignity, on solidarity in community, on the potentially enriching character of culture, and on the "sacredness" of creation. This assault is still more obvious when it is inflicted in the name of God, in other words, when such violence is religiously motivated. Peace, on the contrary, consists not only in the absence of war and/or violence but also and more importantly is the effective expression of a life lived in solidarity with others, with creation, and with God. Thus, peace is inseparable from righteousness and justice.

* * *

Except where otherwise indicated, bold, italics and capitals in quotations are found in the original texts. For the Qur'an, I use *The Meaning of the Noble Qur'an*, electronic edition of July 17, 2006 (at http://www.pdf-koran.com [accessed September 24, 2010]).

Chapter 1

Historical Perspectives on the Religious Justification of Violence

"How beautiful upon the mountains are the feet of the messenger who announces peace, who brings good news, who announces salvation, who says to Zion, 'Your God reigns'" (Isa 52:7). Peace, justice, mercy, solidarity, love, compassion, and forgiveness constitute essential dimensions of the messianic promise of the Hebrew Scriptures (see, for example, Isa 9:1-7; Zech 9:9-10). The God of the promise is, then, a God of peace.

The same proclamation of peace can be found in the New Testament as a fundamental part of Jesus Christ's teaching (see, for example, Mt 5:9). After his resurrection, the first message of Jesus to the Apostles was that peace would be with them (Jn 20:19-29; Lk 24:36). The synoptic gospels, following the Hebrew Scriptures, particularly the prophet Isaiah, put peace together with the arrival of the promised Messiah. Christians recognize in Jesus Christ the fulfillment of this promise. However, Jesus' messianism is very different from the one that was expected: it is not a messianism imposed by force or by violence but by the proclamation of peace.[1] Thus, according to Swartly, "*peace* is [not only] integral to the *gospel* of the kingdom that Jesus proclaimed and brought in his own person,"[2] but also what makes Christians become the "image" of Christ resurrected.[3] The messianism of Jesus implied a deconstruction of the unjust religious and sociopolitical structures of the reigning powers of his time, which were imposed by force and with violence. Jesus' message of peace was not free of conflict, however. When one becomes a peacemaker, a peace in solidarity with justice,[4] one can be confronted with the violence of

[1] See Willard M. Swartly, *Covenant of Peace: The Missing Peace in New Testament Theology and Ethics*, Grand Rapids, Cambridge (UK): William B. Eerdmans Publishing Co., 2006, pp. 15-19, 21-22.

[2] Swartly, *Covenant of Peace*, p. 23.

[3] See Swartly, *Covenant of Peace*, pp. 56-57.

[4] See Swartly, *Covenant of Peace*, p. 143.

those who prefer to maintain the *status quo*.[5] Jesus gave his life to break the *status quo* and confront violence in all of its manifestations.

At the beginning of the Qur'an, and at the start of each Sura[6], is the phrase: "In the name of Allah, Most Gracious, Most Merciful." Graciousness, mercy, compassion and forgiveness are attributes of Allah. Peace, and its wish to others, is also a fundamental part of the message of the Qur'an, as is the case with the two other monotheistic religions: "Peace unto you for that ye persevered in patience! Now how excellent is the final home!" (S 13:24). It is also with the wish of peace, "Peace be upon you," that the faithful Muslim will be received in Paradise (see, for example, S 16:32; 39:73). As in the Hebrew Scriptures and the New Testament, peace is not separated from justice in the Qur'an: "Allah commands justice, the doing of good, and liberality to kith and kin, and He forbids all shameful deeds, and injustice and rebellion: He instructs you, that ye may receive admonition" (S 16:90). As a consequence, Muslims must behave righteously: "To orphans restore their property (When they reach their age), nor substitute (your) worthless things for (their) good ones; and devour not their substance (by mixing it up) with your own. For this is indeed a great sin" (S 4:2; see also 4:135; 5:8).

If peace, justice, and mercy are central to the Holy Scriptures of the three monotheistic religions, how is it possible that these religions have been linked to so much violence and injustice throughout their histories? Violence is present not only in the Hebrew Scriptures, but also in the New Testament and in the Qur'an.[7] It is for this reason that, for many people, monotheism is perceived as the cause of violence: the "one" God becomes jealous and intolerant in front of all other divinities.[8] In reality, it is, however, more likely the intolerance of believers, and the way they have domesticated the Divine, that is at the root of

[5] See Alan Storkey, *Jesus and Politics: Confronting the Powers*, Grand Rapids: Baker Academic, 2005, pp. 125-126, 149-150, 199-200; Walter Wink, *The Powers That Be: Theology for a New Millennium*, New York: Galilee Doubleday, 1998, pp. 112-127.

[6] From now on Sura (Chapter) will be cited with the abbreviation S.

[7] See Pierre Gibert, "L'entrée en Canaan et la violence de Yahvé," in *Le Monde de la Bible*, 194 (2010), pp. 22-27; Jack Nelson-Pallmeyer, *Is Religion Killing Us?: Violence in the Bible and the Quran*, Harrisburg, London (UK), New York: Trinity Press International, 2003, pp. 27-71, 73-94.

[8] See Frédéric Lenoir, "Dieu n'est pas mort pour rien," in *Le Monde des Religions*, 49 (2011), p. 5; Jean-Luc Pouthier, "Au cœur du monothéisme: Le vrai, le faux et la violence," in *Le Monde de la Bible*, 194 (2010), pp. 19-21; Michel Onfray, *Traité d'athéologie: Physique de la métaphysique*, Paris: Bernard Grasset, 2005, pp. 69, 95-96; Thomas Mooren, *War and Peace in Monotheistic Religions*, Delhi: Media House, 2008, pp. 27, 100-103, 124-127.

violence justified in God's name, rather than the God of Abraham, common to all three faiths.

Taking into consideration its cultural and socio-political influences throughout history, we can say that Christianity has often abandoned the "non-violent Jesus of Nazareth."[9] Thus, as Jacques Ellul states, "[w]hat troubles me is that Christians conform to the trend of the moment without introducing into it *anything* specifically Christian. Their convictions are determined by their social milieu, not by faith in revelation; they lack the uniqueness which ought to be the expression of that faith."[10] Nevertheless, for certain theologians, such as the biblical scholar Walter Wink, nonviolence is the core tenet of Christianity and at the heart of Jesus' message.[11]

The seemingly causal relationship between religion and violence is not something exclusive to the three monotheistic religions, however. Lee Griffith highlights this when he writes: "No matter the degree to which tolerance has been encouraged, it must be acknowledged that none of the major religious traditions on the planet has been free from complicity in fostering violence and terror."[12] When we take this acknowledgment into consideration, it is easy enough to understand why so many people today have given up on any kind of religious belief and/or practice.

In this chapter, I will not present the "casual" relationship between religion and violence from a chronological perspective. I would, rather, like to discuss four elements that I believe have contributed to this relationship. First, I analyze how religion moves from being an instrument of social harmony and cultural identity to a source of violence. Second, I examine the tendency to stereotype enemies in order to justify violent behavior against them. Third, I explore some of the violent, even "pathological," images of God found in Holy Scriptures. Fourth, and finally, I address the risk of religion being transformed into "ideology" when engaged with or married to the State, that is, with the powers that be. In this circumstance, religious worship becomes "idolatry," the adoration of a false god.

[9] Hans Küng, *Islam: Past, Present and Future* (J. Bowden, trans.), Oxford (UK): Oneworld Publications (The Religious Situation of our Time, [3]), 2007, p. 308.

[10] Jacques Ellul, *Violence: Reflections from a Christian Perspective* (C. G. Kings, trans.), New York: Seabury Press, 1969, p. 28.

[11] See Wink, *The Powers That Be*, pp. 63-81, 98-111.

[12] Lee Griffith, *The War on Terrorism and the Terror of God*, Grand Rapids, Cambridge (UK): William B. Eerdmans Publishing Co., 2002, p. 61.

1. Religion as an Instrument of Social Harmony and Cultural Identity

Violence, according to René Girard, is the foundational dimension of ancient cultures. As Mack C. Stirling summarizes, "Girard postulates that human culture originated in the violent murder of a human being, *the scapegoat.*"[13] The "mimetic desires," that lead people to want what the other person desires are at the origin of violence, both at personal and social levels.[14] The community reaches a state of harmony and can live in collective peace by projecting onto an innocent "propitiatory victim" the tendency to eliminate the other person for possessing the objects of other's desires.[15] Thus, "[t]he hatred directed toward the scapegoat unites members of the community. They forget their antagonisms, and the violent emotions that they have had for one another are projected into the surrogate victim. Everyone becomes united in desiring the same negative–the destruction of the scapegoat."[16] Following this mythic interpretation found in socio-cultural anthropology, Girard proposes that the function of religion was to avoid violence becoming a destructive element in society. In almost all ancient religions, there existed a scapegoat onto whom the society's collective violence was projected. After its sacrificial death, the scapegoat was divinized by the same community, transformed into its savior, the foundation of morality and, as a result, the

[13] Mack C. Stirling, "Violent Religion: René Girard's Theory of Culture," in J. Harold Ellens (Ed.), *The Destructive Power of Religion: Violence in Judaism, Christianity, and Islam*, vol. 2 (Religion, Psychology, and Violence), Westport, Connecticut, London (UK): Praeger (Contemporary Psychology), 2004, p. 23; see also pp. 24-36; René Girard, *Je vois Satan tomber comme l'éclair*, Paris: Bernard Grasset, 1999, p. 133.

[14] See Girard, *Je vois Satan tomber comme l'éclair*, pp. 27-36.

[15] According to René Girard, this tendency is found "everywhere" in mythology (see *Je vois Satan tomber comme l'éclair*, p. 11).

[16] Vernon Neufeld Redekop, *From Violence to Blessing: How an Understanding of Deep-Rooted Conflict Can Open Paths to Reconciliation*, Ottawa: Novalis, 2002, p. 99. Analyzing contemporary conflicts, Redekop underlies further the importance of hidden mechanisms: "Hegemonic structural analysis of deep-rooted conflict exposes hidden patterns that have a strong psychological impact on individuals and groups. These patterns reinforce feelings of shame and entitlement in both 'oppressed' and 'oppressors'" (p. 120; see also Ricardo J. Quinones, "The Cain-Abel Syndrome: In Theory and in History," in J. Harold Ellens [Ed.], *The Destructive Power of Religion: Violence in Judaism, Christianity, and Islam*, vol. 3 [Models and Cases of Violence in Religion], Westport, Connecticut, London (UK): Praeger [Contemporary Psychology], 2004, pp. 81-125). In this regard, a few years before the publication of his book, Redekop highlighted how, according to Girard, the "scapegoat mechanism" is something hidden. In other words, "people are never, ever aware of the fact that they are making a scapegoat of someone" (*Scapegoats, the Bible, and Criminal Justice: Interacting with René Girard*, Akron: Mennonite Central Committee [Issue no. 13], 1993, p. 14).

guarantor of order and peace.[17] For this reason, and from this anthropological perspective, religions are linked to the origin of ancient cultures as being an essential element in social harmony.

Religions have been, and still are, instruments of cultural identity. The psychological and sociological power of religion as an organizing cultural factor that gives meaning to the person and to society is well documented.[18] At the same time, and contrary to this positive dimension, the cultural identity that is fostered by religion can be manipulated for selfish interests through violence.[19] In the process of identity formation, people oftentimes become aware of their specific cultural and religious identities not by looking to other's people identities as a source of inspiration but as a threat against them: "We are not them," "Our God is not their God," "Our religion is not their religion." Thus, as Díez de Velasco points out, "[a] religious construction of identity and otherness can turn the different into a scapegoat, whose disappearance or annihilation is considered the solution to the problem."[20] Therefore, in contradiction with the function of maintaining peace, social harmony and cultural identity, religions also carry within them the potential of becoming contributors to violence and to the processes of demonizing others, their beliefs and their cultural characteristics.

[17] See Girard, *Je vois Satan tomber comme l'éclair*, p. 113; see also Redekop, *Scapegoats, the Bible, and Criminal Justice*, p. 15.

[18] See Marc Gopin, *Between Eden and Armageddon: The Future of World Religions, Violence and Peacemaking*, Oxford (UK), Toronto: Oxford University Press, 2000, p. 13; James K. Wellmand, Jr., and Kyoko Tokuno, "Is Religious Violence Inevitable?," in *Journal for the Scientific Study of Religion*, 43/3 (2004), p. 292; Francisco Díez de Velasco, "Theoretical Reflections on Violence and Religion: Identity, Power, Privilege and Difference (With Reference to the Hispanic World)," in *Numen*, 52 (2005), p. 90.

[19] See Paul N. Anderson, "Religion and Violence: From Pawn to Scapegoat," in Ellens (Ed.), *The Destructive Power of Religion*, vol. 2, pp. 265-283.

[20] Díez de Velasco, "Theoretical Reflections on Violence and Religion," p. 91. Wellman, Jr., and Tokuno say in this regard: "We argue, therefore, that it is a part of the nature of religious communities to gain their identity through conflict and tension with out-group cultures. Conflict, in this sense, is socially functional. Identity is galvanized by the degree to which one is against the outsider, the other, whether as a competing religious community or a powerful national regime.... It is against these external forces that they portray their purity, as with Protestantism; their chosenness, as with the Jews; their single-mindedness, as with Islam; or their clarity, as with the Sri Lankan Buddhists. This tension and conflict with out-groups does not always lead to violence" ("Is Religious Violence Inevitable?," p. 292). In the same sense, Oliver J. McTernan points out: "From Indonesia to Northern Ireland, the Middle East to Kashmir, India to Nigeria, the Balkans to Sri Lanka, Christian, Buddhist, Jews, Hindus, Muslims and Sikhs justify the use of violence on the grounds that they are protecting their religious identity and interest" (*Violence in God's Name: Religion in an Age of Conflict*, Maryknoll: Orbis Books, 2003, p. ix).

2. Demonization of the Other

Mark Juergensmeyer states: "[E]nemies have to be invented if they do not already exist.... Put simply, one cannot have a war without an enemy."[21] Not only is there a need to invent enemies but there is also a need to stereotype and demonize them.[22] This resulting negative perception provides an apparent justification for acting violently against so-called enemies, as I will discuss in the next chapter.[23]

Dualistic, Manichean, and apocalyptic conceptions of the world, of us being good and others being bad, is also a constant in the history of humanity. In this understanding of the world, God is on "our" side against others, and "our" God will triumph over "our" enemies.[24] As a consequence, the enemy's faults are magnified but the faults of "God's chosen" are quickly passed over.[25] Yet, this dualistic and Manichaeistic epistemology of good against evil is antithetically opposed to the Judeo-Christian vision of the world. As J. Harold Ellens insists, it is "profoundly untrue."[26] The essential message of Jesus Christ is the love of

[21] Mark Juergensmeyer, *Terror in the Mind of God: The Global Rise of Religious Violence* (Updated edition with a new preface), Berkeley, Los Angeles, London (UK): University of California Press (Comparative Studies in Religion and Society, 13), 2001 (©2000), p. 171.

[22] See Juergensmeyer, *Terror in the Mind of God*, p. 172. A few pages later, he develops further his argumentation on the process of demonization of enemies: "I call this process satanization. The process of creating satanic enemies is part of the construction of an image of cosmic war, and some of the same criteria listed at the end of the previous chapter that make sacred warfare possible also make possible a satanic opponent. When the opponent rejects one's moral or spiritual position; when the enemy appears to hold the power to completely annihilate one's community, one's culture, and oneself; when the opponent's victory would be unthinkable; and when there seems no way to defeat the enemy in human terms–all of these conditions increase the likelihood that one will envision one's opponent as a superhuman foe, a cosmic enemy. The process of satanization is aimed at reducing the power of one's opponents and discrediting them. By belittling and humiliating them–by making them subhuman–one is asserting one's own superior moral power" (pp. 182-183).

[23] See Myriam Vaucher, "Vie, violence...: La haine, voie de transformation de la violence," in Daniel Marguerat (Ed.), *Dieu est-il violent?*, Paris: Bayard Édition, 2008, p. 14.

[24] See Jack Nelson-Pallmeyer, *Jesus against Christianity: Reclaiming the Missing Jesus*, Harrisburg, Pennsylvania: Trinity Press International, 2001, p. 183. For his part, Lee Griffith points out: "The theme of ethical dualism in which the armies of 'light' oppose the armies of 'darkness' emerges with alarming frequency from church history" (*The War on Terrorism and the Terror of God*, p. 100).

[25] See Nelson-Pallmeyer, *Is Religion Killing Us?*, pp. 112-113.

[26] J. Harold Ellens, "Introduction: The Destructive Power of Religion," in J. Harold Ellens (Ed.), *The Destructive Power of Religion: Violence in Judaism, Christianity, and Islam*, vol. 1 (Sacred Scriptures, Ideology, and Violence), Westport, Connecticut, London (UK): Praeger (Contemporary Psychology), 2004, p. 3; see also p. 4.

one's enemies (see, for example, Mt 5:43-48; Lk 6:27-36). Enemies can reveal to believers dimensions of themselves that they do not care to recognize or simply cannot see.[27] This revelation implies the need for a self-conscious analysis on the part of believers:

> It is clear... that not seeing the logs in our own eyes is costly for ourselves and others. Salvation and God's favor can no longer be understood as defeat of enemies, as much of the Bible and Quran suggests. Among salvation's prominent meanings are healing and wholeness for individuals, communities, and the world itself. Vilifying enemies and militarizing conflicts legitimated by appeals to "sacred" texts escalate a spiral of violence. In this sense, as Jesus suggested, we truly are saved by our enemies. Because our "sacred" texts legitimate violence, we must also be saved by doubt.[28]

The possibility of being "saved by our enemies," by those who reveal to us important dimensions of "ourselves," requires entering into a different process of identity formation. We become ourselves not by opposition to others but in relationship to them and with them. Others are mirrors that reflect back to us our deepest characteristics. Demonizing others not only destroys them, but also ourselves: we dehumanize ourselves as we dehumanize others.

In order to overcome the process of demonizing others, believers need to overcome and free themselves from the "pathological portraits of God" that justify violence against them.

3. "Pathological Portraits of God"

Religions have often legitimized the image of a vindictive God: a ruthless judge rather than someone who loves unconditionally; a judge who monitors believers and keeps a record of all their bad attitudes and actions in lieu of a final Day of Judgment.[29] God is often enough presented as a "warrior and cruel" Divinity who justifies alienation and violence.

It is beyond the scope of this study to cite all the sacred texts of the three monotheistic religions which present such "pathological portraits

[27] See Redekop, *From Violence to Blessing*, p. 29; Wink, *The Powers That Be*, pp. 161, 170-171.

[28] Nelson-Pallmeyer, *Is Religion Killing Us?*, p. 126.

[29] See Ramón Martínez de Pisón, *Life beyond Death: The Eschatological Dimension of Christian Faith*, Ottawa: Novalis, 2007, pp. 24-25.

of God." However, Jack Nelson-Pallmeyer applies to these images of God the psychological characteristics for determining if a behavior, or person, is pathological.[30] According to his criteria, there is no doubt that some of God's interventions, as they are reflected in the Hebrew Scriptures and the New Testament, can be considered as pathological.

Some of the texts, to which Nelson-Pallmeyer refers, from the Hebrew Scriptures are God's announcement to Noah of the destruction of the Earth because of its corruption (Gen 6:11-22), and the accomplishment of this destruction by the Great Flood (Gen 7); the commandment to Abraham to sacrifice his son Isaac (Gen 22:1-19);[31] and the authorization of the death penalty for offering human sacrifices to the idols (Lev 20:1-2). Other texts speak of the human sacrifice of Jephthah's daughter to God as an offering in exchange for the victory of the Israelites against the Am'mon·ītes (Judg 11); God's order to Moses to "avenge the Israelites" against Midian (Num 31); the mass murder or genocide of the invaded people (Deut 7:1-2. 5-6); the order to kill some small boys jeering at the prophet Elijah (2 Kings 2:23-24); and the cruel, angered and choleric God who proclaims war against Babylon (Isa 13) and the punishment of Zion (Lam 4).[32]

We also find several "pathological portraits" in the New Testament. As Nelson-Pallmeyer underscores, "[t]he New Testament is filled with images of God consistent with the pathology of God described earlier based on Hebrew scriptural accounts."[33] For example, the celebrations

[30] See Nelson-Pallmeyer, *Jesus against Christianity*, pp. 24-62; Nelson-Pallmeyer, *Is Religion Killing Us?*, pp. 27-94.

[31] See Yvonne Sherwood, "Binding–Unbinding: Divided Responses of Judaism, Christianity, and Islam to the 'Sacrifice' of Abraham's Beloved Son," in *Journal of the American Academy of Religion*, 72/4 (2004), pp. 821-861; Donald Capp "Abraham and Isaac: The Sacrificial Impulse," in Ellens (Ed.), *The Destructive Power of Religion*, vol. 1, pp. 169-189.

[32] See André Wénin, "'Adonaï est un guerrier' (Ex 15, 3): La violence divine dans le premier Testament," in Jean Daniel Causse, Élian Cuvillier and André Wénin, *Divine violence: Approche exégétique et anthropologique*, Paris: Éditions du Cerf, Médiaspaul (Lire la Bible, 168), 2011, pp. 15-66.

[33] Nelson-Pallmeyer, *Jesus against Christianity*, p. 57. A few pages later, it is stated that: "The pathology of God described extensively in reference to the Hebrew Scriptures is firmly attested within the New Testament as well" (p. 61). Besides, as J. Harold Ellens points out, we find in the New Testament scenes of what he considers to be Jesus' own violent behavior, as, for example, the cleansing of the temple (Jn 2:13-25); chastising his mother at the wedding in Cana (Jn 2:1-4); reprimanding Peter (Mk 8:31-33) and exploiting the blind man in John 9 (see "Introduction: Spiral of Violence," in J. Harold Ellens [Ed.], *The Destructive Power of Religion: Violence in Judaism, Christianity, and Islam*, vol. 4 [Contemporary Views on Spirituality and Violence], Westport, Connecticut, London [UK]: Praeger [Contemporary Psychology], 2004, pp. 1-17). In this

of "the Feast of Passover that commemorates the defeat of Israel's enemies;"[34] the image of God which appears in Mary's song of praise (Lk 1:51-53); the one in the story of the healing of the Gerasene demoniac (Mk 5:9-13); the deadly punishment of Ananias and Sapphira (Acts 5:1-11) and innumerable seemingly violent passages in Revelation (see, for example, 6:9-10; 9:13-15; 11:17-18; 14:9-11; 21:8); without mentioning the image of the Final Judgment of the Nations (Mt 25:31-46) and the many texts on the punishment of the damned in Hell for all of eternity. All of this, without forgetting the passages where some particular Jewish groups appear more or less demonized and responsible for Jesus Christ's death, and the prejudices and violence against Jewish people in general, which these narratives have caused throughout the history of Christianity.[35]

As a conclusion to his presentation of biblical images of a sadistic, pathological God, Nelson-Pallmeyer writes:

> The biblical portraits of God as murderous, wrathful, hateful, and venomous are so widespread that they leave us no choice but to cross out parts of the Bible, not through disingenuous silent censorship but through conscious choices guided by clear and transparent criteria. We must read the Bible with eyes wide open. When human beings invoke God's name, or write about God, or describe what God is like, we must judge whether God is really being talked about. The pathological portraits of God painted by the biblical writers force us to be discerning readers, with the life and faith of Jesus as our guide.[36]

Given Nelson-Pallmeyer's reasoning, it is understandable why scholars such as Maurice Bellet, a French Roman Catholic priest, wrote a book

regard, Maurice Bellet, speaking about the "absolute violence," that is to say, the violence that has God as agent, says how this "absolute violence" is a creation of Christianity. Thus, "this perverse Christianity will be the fulfillment of such absolute violence" (*"Je ne suis pas venu apporter la paix..."*: *Essai sur la violence absolue*, Paris: Éditions Albin Michel, 2009, pp. 88-89 [my translation]). According to what he says in the next pages of this book, we are not only in the presence of a perversion of Christianity, but of a Christ who appears, as many other images of God in Holy Scriptures, as a "perverse" Christ who is the incarnated expression of "absolute violence" (see pp. 90-91). However, in Chapter 5, I will present how, in fact, Jesus Christ's revelation of God signifies a deconstruction of these "pathological portraits of God." This deconstruction is in fact the intention of Nelson-Pallmeyer and Bellet in their studies.

[34] Nelson-Pallmeyer, *Jesus against Christianity*, p. 55.

[35] See Élian Cuvillier, "Violence des hommes, violence de Dieu: Regard sur quelques texts du Nouveau Testament," in Causse, Cuvillier and Wénin, *Divine violence*, pp. 99-173.

[36] Nelson-Pallmeyer, *Jesus against Christianity*, p. 62.

that became famous in 1998, *Le Dieu pervers* (*The Perverse God*).[37] For Bellet, God really appears as depraved, perverse, and pathological. This is often how theological reflection has presented God: as forbidding "critical thinking" and everything that is pleasurable and makes life joyful. This is the case not only with some of the images of God in the Hebrew Scriptures but also with Jesus Christ who appears as "the great masochist," the summit of "the perverse God." In Christian tradition there exists the image of a divine Father who rejoices in the suffering of his own son. It is here that there is rooted the development of a spirituality based on offering suffering to God, a spirituality that fosters mortification and martyrdom. Suffering is understood as having a redemptive value, bringing believers closer to Jesus' own suffering and death.[38] As Saint Augustine (354–430) says in his *Sermon on Shepherds*: "Christians are meant to imitate Christ's sufferings, not to go seeking pleasure."[39]

Therefore, Jesus' suffering is understood as an example to be followed. This tendency belongs to a tradition that goes back to the New Testament itself, as can be seen in the Letter of Saint Paul to the Colossians (1:24). Such an understanding of suffering contributed to an unhealthy acceptance of it, particularly of the suffering inflicted on the innocent. This is a very limited and theologically controversial interpretation of "redemptive suffering" and its application to Jesus' own and to various contemporary examples of suffering, as I discuss further on in the present study. As a result, there is a need for us now to overcome any such reductive and distorted understanding of God and of suffering that suggests suffering is something willed by God for spiritual maturation and happiness. This is an erroneous notion inherited from the past which, in large measure, remains present and influential in many theological interpretations of images of God in the Bible.

The Qur'an also carries with it distorted and pathological images of Allah who appears as a warrior and vengeful God,[40] as is illustrated by S 2:216: "Fighting is prescribed for you, and ye dislike it. But it is possible that ye dislike a thing which is good for you, and that ye love a thing

[37] See Maurice Bellet, *Le Dieu pervers* (Nouvelle édition), Paris: Desclée de Brower, 2002 (©1998); see also Bellet, *"Je ne suis pas venu apporter la paix…"*, p. 42.

[38] See Bellet, *Le Dieu pervers*, pp. 71-72.

[39] Aurelius Augustinus, *Sermons: II (20–50) on the Old Testament* (E. Hill, trans. and notes; J. E. Rotelle [Ed.]), Brooklyn: New City Press (The Work of Saint Augustine: A translation for the 21st Century, 3), 1990, Sermon 46, number 10, p. 269.

[40] See Denis Gril, "L'islam prône-t-il la violence?," in *Le Monde de la Bible*, 194 (2010), pp. 34-36; Nelson-Pallmeyer, *Is Religion Killing Us?*, pp. 73-94.

which is bad for you. But Allah knoweth, and ye know not." A similar image is given in S 4:84: "Then fight in Allah's cause–Thou art held responsible only for thyself–and rouse the believers. It may be that Allah will restrain the fury of the Unbelievers; for Allah is the strongest in might and in punishment."[41] In S 47:4, believers read:

> Therefore, when ye meet the Unbelievers (in fight), smite at their necks; At length, when ye have thoroughly subdued them, bind a bond firmly (on them): thereafter (is the time for) either generosity or ransom: Until the war lays down its burdens. Thus (are ye commanded): but if it had been Allah' Will, He could certainly have exacted retribution from them (Himself); but (He lets you fight) in order to test you, some with others. But those who are slain in the Way of Allah, He will never let their deeds be lost.

When monotheistic religions support these distorted images of God and enter into a covenant with the State, they risk falling into "the triumph of ideology."[42] In this circumstance, worship in these traditions risks becoming "idolatry" and religion itself too easily devolves into a mere projection of human and partisan political interests rather than serving as a vehicle that mediates an encounter with the Divine.

4. Marriage between Religion and State: "The Triumph of Ideology"

In the West, the separation of religion and State is something quite recent. Until the French Revolution (1789–1799), it was inconceivable for a State and its people to be without a more formal religion. In this regard, before the Revolution religion was considered as a "national matter," allying itself with the State. In many instances, this alliance transformed the State into a theocratic institution.

This tendency to marry religion and the State, indeed religion and politics, can already be seen in the Hebrew Scriptures. Here, the link between religion and Empire "distorted both Jewish expectations of God's future action and Gospel portraits of Jesus."[43] In this context,

[41] See also S 8:15-17. 67; 9:12-14. 38-39; 33: 25-27; 46:27.

[42] I use the term "ideology" as the projection of a particular conviction as having an absolute, universal, value. In this sense, "[t]he proper nature of an ideology is that it is a conviction which is believed to be evoked by reality but is in fact kept alive by the desire to satisfy individual interests.... Ideology will always tend toward onesidedness" (Concilium General Secretariat, "Utopia," in *Concilium*, 5/1 [1969], p. 77).

[43] Nelson-Pallmeyer, *Jesus against Christianity*, p. 176; see also p. 179.

Judaism became a vehicle of oppression, and faith in a God of justice and compassion nearly disappeared.[44]

Similarly, Alistair Kee highlights how Christianity was transformed into an ideology once it became the official religion of the Roman Empire under Constantine (272–337). In this regard, Kee presents a radical opposition between the Emperor and Jesus Christ, and notes that the Church took advantage of the support of Constantine. Kee vehemently denies the authenticity, or the sincerity, of Constantine's conversion to Christianity. According to him, "Constantine was a devotee of the God of the Christians. But that was not the same as being a Christian."[45] Constantine's attitude toward Christianity was motivated more by political reasons than for personal convictions. Despite the positive attitude of the Church toward the Emperor, rooted in the end of the persecutions against Christians and the privileged position given to Christianity in the Empire, Kee argues that Constantine's ideology triumphed over the Gospel.[46] What is important here is not so much the way in which Constantine was converted to Christianity, "but how through his religious policy he succeeded in converting Christianity to his position."[47] According to Kee,

[44] See Nelson-Pallmeyer, *Jesus against Christianity*, p. 197. Following on, on the same page, one reads: "The imperial situation meant collaborating Jews were incapable of upholding a justice tradition. This was true for high priests, aristocratic families, and midlevel retainers alike. None could truly defend widows and orphans, break cycles of indebtedness, insure rights to and fair distribution of God's land, or rule in light of the sovereignty of God as parts of the Torah and other aspects of the tradition demanded. Why? Because satisfying Rome and securing their own positions of power depended on faithful exploitation of the people. Pleasing Rome, defending their own privileges, and in some cases plain survival, necessarily led to exploitation of the people and to distortion of God, Temple, and Torah.

"Only part of the blame for oppressive rule can be laid at the feet of the Romans, however. During times of independent rule, Jewish elites often oppressed the people and distorted God and scripture in pursuit of wealth, power and other privileges [Isa 3:14-15]."

[45] Alistair Kee, *Constantine versus Christ: The Triumph of Ideology*, London (UK): SCM Press Ltd., 1982, p. 23.

[46] See Kee, *Constantine versus Christ*, pp. 88, 101-102.

[47] Kee, *Constantine versus Christ*, p. 115. Kee highlights, not without irony, the fact that the religious influence of Constantine had continued without problems throughout centuries in the Western culture. Obery M. Hendricks, Jr., points out as well how the confusion between religion and politics, which was initiated with Constantine, continued to be present long after him: "This confusion of militarism and political domination with the cause of Christ continues throughout the subsequent history of the West. The Crusades, the Inquisition, the Holocaust, the genocidal 'missionary' campaigns against the native peoples of the Americas, and the cruel enslavement of human beings in the 'Christian' United States are only a few examples" (*The Politics of Jesus: Rediscovering the True Revolutionary Nature of the Teaching of Jesus and How They Have Been Corrupted*, New York: Doubleday, 2006, p. 87).

Constantine displaced Jesus Christ, transforming himself into the awaited savior.[48] The influence of Christianity in the history and culture of Europe depended greatly, therefore, on the game into which Constantine forced the Church to enter.[49] As a result, "Christ remains at the centre of Christianity, but the values of the historical Jesus are now replaced by the values of Constantine. This is seen nowhere more dramatically than in Byzantine art, in which Christ is represented as seated in a heaven which looks suspiciously like Constantine's court in Byzantium."[50] This situation continued in the Church for centuries. Jesus Christ and his central message of justice and peace disappeared from the religious landscape. His ethical radicalism also vanished:

> Christian churches across the theological and confessional spectrum, and Christian ethics as an academic discipline that serves the churches, are often guilty of evading Jesus, the cornerstone and center of Christian faith. Specifically, *the teaching and practices of Jesus*–especially the largest block of his teachings, the Sermon on the Mount–are routinely ignored or misinterpreted in the preaching and teaching ministry of the churches and in Christian scholarship in ethics. This evasion of the concrete teachings of Jesus has seriously malformed Christian moral practices, moral beliefs and moral witness.[51]

The ideological deformation of the Gospel, from Constantine on, has accompanied Western Christianity throughout history.[52] Although once persecuted themselves, Christians often became the persecutors when Christianity became the established official religion of the Roman Empire under Theodosius the Great, Emperor from 379 to 395.[53] The "State religion" into which Christianity was transformed privileged the clergy who personally benefited from the changes. Bishops became officials of the Empire. With the decline of the Western Roman Empire (476), bishops, including the bishop of Rome, assumed the role of both

[48] See Kee, *Constantine versus Christ*, pp. 123-127.

[49] See Kee, *Constantine versus Christ*, pp. 140-141, 157, 159.

[50] Kee, *Constantine versus Christ*, p. 153; see also François Dermange, "Toute-puissance divine et toute-puissance politique: Une symétrie ambiguë," in Marguerat (Ed.), *Dieu est-il violent?*, pp. 106-111.

[51] Glen Harold Stassen and David P. Gushee, *Kingdom Ethics: Following Jesus in Contemporary Context*, Downers Grove: InterVarsity Press, 2003, p. 11.

[52] See Hendricks, *The Politics of Jesus*, p. 87.

[53] See Grant R. Shafer, "Hell, Martyrdom, and War: Violence in Early Christianity," in Ellens (Ed.), *The Destructive Power of Religion*, vol. 3, pp. 193-246; Mooren, *War and Peace in Monotheistic Religions*, pp. 15-16, 50-64; Robert A. Markus, *Christianity and the Secular*, Notre Dame: University of Notre Dame Press (Blessed Pope John XXIII Lecture Series in Theology and Culture), 2006, p. 21.

religious and political leaders.[54] During the Middle Ages (5th–15th Centuries), the Pope combined spiritual and temporal power resulting in an almost total meshing of these powers: "Throughout the twelfth and the thirteenth centuries," says Rapley, "the papacy was the closest thing then in existence to a pan-European power."[55] The price that Christianity has paid as a result of so many centuries of privilege and the use of violence for its own interest, as shown by the Crusades, the Inquisition, and so many other examples, has been enormous. The decline of imperial Christianity carried with it, on the part of many Christians, a turning away from the Churches rooted in those Christians becoming ever more conscious of the value of the person and of freedom.[56]

In contrast with the case of Christianity, which was "forced" to accept a divorce from the State and to enter into a process of socio-political secularization, in Judaism[57] and, particularly in Islam,[58] there remains a covenant between religion and the State, between religion and political power. This was already clear in the life of the prophet Muhammad in whom it is very difficult to separate being the vehicle of the "last" revelation of Allah from the statesman.[59]

I fully agree with the position of Hans Küng that a separation of religion and the State is an issue in all the monotheistic traditions. He says that "[t]he question of the unity or separation of religion and state is a problem for all three prophetic religions: a problem which poses itself in different ways at different periods of history and which has led to a diversity of models of this relationship with different nuances."[60] As I will say in Chapter 6 below, I do not, however, understand this separation as an opposition or a lack of collaboration between religion and the State.

* * *

[54] See Elizabeth Rapley, *The Lord as Their Portion: The Story of the Religious Orders and How They Shaped Our World*, Grand Rapids, Toronto: William B. Eerdmans Publishing Co., Novalis, 2011, pp. 6-7.

[55] Rapley, *The Lord as Their Portion*, p. 54; see also pp. 51-53.

[56] See Claude Michaud, "Vers un au-delà de la violence faite à l'intelligence des catholiques," in Pierre Noël (Ed.), *Mondialisation, violence et religion*, Montréal: Fides (Hétirage et Projet, 74), 2009, p. 163.

[57] See Küng, *Islam*, pp. 580-581.

[58] See Charles T. Davis III, "The Qur'an, Muhammad, and Jihad in Context," in Ellens (Ed.), *The Destructive Power of Religion*, vol. 1, p. 241; Küng, *Islam*, p. 585.

[59] See Irving M. Zeitlin, *The Historical Muhammad*, Cambridge (UK): Polity Press, 2008 (©2007), pp. 154-164.

[60] Küng, *Islam*, p. 580; see also pp. 578, 585-587.

In this chapter, I have moved from considering religion as an instrument of peace, social harmony and cultural identity, to its deformation and transformation into an ideology that justifies violence. This process was made possible by a double manipulation: the demonization of the other–stereotyping the enemy; and, the projection of morbid human tendencies onto the Divine, giving God an almost "pathological" appearance.

This is a process experienced in each of the three monotheistic religions. Contrary to the proclamation of peace, justice and mercy, that can be found at the heart of Judaism, Christianity, and Islam, these religions have been transformed, in great measure, into sources of violence. This is a situation that, as I explore in the next chapter, is still very much present.

Based on the discussions examined in this chapter, a first conclusion about the link between religion and violence can be drawn: religion is not, by itself alone, a source of violence. The religious justification of violence finds its roots in human manipulation. As a result, God is no longer understood as the transcendent Other who calls believers to live a full life, and calls them to a personal transformation in solidarity with other human beings and with creation. God is transformed into a domesticated Divinity made into humanity's "own image" and put into the service of selfish human interests.

Chapter 2

Contemporary Violence in the Name of Yahweh, Jesus Christ, and Allah

Unfortunately we do not have to look far to find evidence of violence and conflict committed in the name of the Divine. We are inundated by it every day in the television news or on internet blogs. This violence to which we refer does not manifest itself naturally in life, nor does it emerge from an uncontrolled drive or instinct (as postulated by Sigmund Freud [1856–1939]).[1] It is, rather, a form of violence whose sole aim is annihilation–of others and ultimately of creation.[2] As Mark Juergensmeyer says:

> Religion seems to be connected with violence virtually everywhere. Since this book was first published [2000], religious violence has erupted among right-wing Christians in the United States, angry Muslims and Jews in the Middle East, quarrelling Hindus and Muslims in South Asia, and indigenous religious communities in Africa and Indonesia. Like the activists associated with Osama bin Laden [1957–2011], the individuals involved in these cases have also relied on religion to provide political identities and give license to vengeful ideologies.[3]

What is significant here is not only that violence is omnipresent in our world but that it has also become in a way the dominant form of religion, as will be discussed here below in the first part of this chapter. However, what is more outrageous is that one of the most lethal forms of violence today is the violence inflicted in the name of God. I examine

[1] See Jean Daniel Causse, "La violence archaïque et le paradoxe du sacrifice aux dieux obscurs," in Causse, Cuvillier and Wénin, *Divine violence*, pp. 67-98.

[2] See Daniel Marguerat, "Préface," in Marguerat (Ed.), *Dieu est-il violent?*, p. 8.

[3] Juergensmeyer, *Terror in the Mind of God*, p. xi; see also p. xii. In another publication, Juergensmeyer returns to the same topic of contemporary religious violence in other places in the world. He states: "What unites these disparate acts of violence is their perpetrators' hatred of the global reach of the modern secular state" (Mark Juergensmeyer, "Religious Terror and Global War," in Bryan Rennie and Philip L. Tite [Eds.], *Religion, Terror and Violence: Religious Studies Perspectives*, New York, London [UK]: Routledge, 2008, p. 129). In Chapter 6 below, I will return to this issue, namely, complaints on behalf of religious terrorists that "modern secular states" do not possess any "values" as a justification for violence against Western countries.

this form of violence in the second part of the present chapter here below. Those who wrongfully use God's name to justify their violent behavior consider themselves called by God to execute a kind of "divine" mandate. I call this "the Redeemer complex." Finally, in the third part of the present chapter, I challenge the morality of what is called "proactive or preemptive defense" and/or "retaliation." I do so while recognizing the legitimate right to defend oneself or one's country against external aggression.

1. Violence: "The Dominant Religion"

For Nelson-Pallmeyer, violence has become the dominant religion in the world today. He writes:

> Violence today is God, the one and only functional God at the heart of most ideologies, whether capitalist, Marxist, anarchist, revolutionary, reactionary, or religious. In the secular world, superior violence is God because violence is presumed to be the only and ultimate means to security or victory or revenge.[4]

Walter Wink echoes this understanding when he refers to what he calls "the myth of redemptive violence." This myth consists of "the belief that violence saves, that war brings peace, that might makes right. It is one of the oldest continuously repeated stories in the world."[5] In another publication, he suggests that violence has become a spirituality in contemporary Western society.[6] The transformation of violence into a spirituality is dangerous because it normalizes violence. Violence becomes the ultimate reason for religious piety and the most efficient way of deterring future aggressors. Wink states that, because this spirituality has become so routine, it has been accepted with equal enthusiasm across conservative and liberal religious divides.

Within this mythic interpretation of violence, war is transformed and sublimated into a kind of spiritual experience that can be understood as essential for saving a population in moral collapse. Based on

[4] Nelson-Pallmeyer, *Is Religion Killing Us?*, p. 136; see also Walter Wink, *Engaging the Powers: Discernment and Resistance in a World of Domination*, Minneapolis: Fortress Press, 1992, p. 13; Wink, *The Power That Be*, pp. 37-62.

[5] Wink, *The Power That Be*, p. 42.

[6] See Walter Wink, "The Myth of Redemptive Violence," in Ellens (Ed.), *The Destructive Power of Religion*, vol. 3, p. 265. He asks why there is such a myth, and he answers: "because it is the conviction that only violence can save us" (p. 266).

his experiences as a war journalist, Chris Hedges testifies that, "[w]ar makes the world understandable, a black and white tableau of them and us. It suspends thought, especially self-critical thought."[7] Following upon Karl Marx (1818–1883)'s critique of religion as the "opium of the people,"[8] I consider violence as being transformed, for many people, into a "new opium," that is to say, into a kind of drug for avoiding reality–particularly painful events. Hedges emphasizes this point:

> I learned early on that war forms its own culture. The rush of battle is a potent and often lethal addiction, for war is a drug, one I ingested for many years.... It dominates culture, distorts memory, corrupts language, and infects everything around it, even humor, which becomes preoccupied with the grim perversities of smut and death. Fundamental questions about the meaning, or meaninglessness, of our place on the planet are laid bare when we watch those around us sink to the lowest depths. War exposes the capacity for evil that lurks not far below the surface within all of us. And this is why for many war is so hard to discuss once it is over.[9]

Violence, then, is experienced as an empowerment, though often disproportionately greater than the violence used to achieve such a sense of power.[10] This experience of empowerment infuses into terrorism "an element of calculation, an effort to generate and harness the irrational whirlwind of human fear. Terror*ism* is the intentional effort to generate fear through violence or the threat of violence and the further effort to harness these fears in pursuit of some goal."[11] Through terrorist actions,

[7] Chris Hedges, *War Is a Force that Gives Us Meaning*, New York: Anchor Books, 2003 (©2002), p. 10. It is hard, but interesting, to read what he says on the previous page: "The eruption of conflict instantly reduces the headache and trivia of daily life. The communal march against an enemy generates a warm, unfamiliar bond with our neighbors, our community, our nation, wiping out unsettling undercurrents of alienation and dislocation. War, in times of malaise and desperation, is a potent distraction" (p. 9). Later on, speaking about the seduction of battle and the perversion of war transformed into an entertainment, he adds: "The violent breakup of Yugoslavia, which was preceded by economic collapse, began in 1991. It was the same year that the government decided to permit hard-core sex films to be broadcast on public stations and the first locally made pornographic film was produced.... The war was, like the sex films, about the lifting of taboos, about new forms of entertainment to mask the economic and political collapse of Yugoslavia. War and sex were the stimulus to divert a society that was collapsing" (pp. 98-99). I will deal with violence as a "distraction" or "entertainment" in Chapter 4, when speaking about Western culture.

[8] See Karl Marx, *Economic and Philosophic Manuscripts of 1844* (M. Milligan, trans.), Moscow: Foreign Languages Publication House, 1961.

[9] Hedges, *War Is a Force that Gives Us Meaning*, p. 3.

[10] See Juergensmeyer, *Terror in the Mind of God*, p. 188-191.

[11] Griffith, *The War on Terrorism and the Terror of God*, p. 6.

people feel powerful by dominating others. In this circumstance, terrorism can take on the aura of a mysticism, a kind of negative spirituality that engenders death rather than fostering life. For this reason, violence appears both indispensable and inevitable.[12] However, Jacques Ellul adds that this is precisely what should make people "reject and oppose it."[13]

Another dimension that is present in contemporary religious violence is the fact that those who use the Divine for justifying their violent actions are manipulating the name of God. I discuss the dangers of this manipulation in the following section.

2. Wrongful Use of God's Name: The Redeemer Complex

"You shall not make wrongful use of the name of the LORD your God, for the LORD will not acquit anyone who misuses his name" (Ex 20:7; see also Deut 5:11). In spite of the Divine interdiction against it, as expressed in the Decalogue (the Ten Commandments) of the Hebrew Scriptures, God's name is one of the most manipulated of all names. Martin Buber (1878–1965) underlines this manipulation:

> [God] is the most heavy-laden of all human words. None has become so soiled, so mutilated.... Generations of men [and women] have laid the burden of their anxious lives upon this word and weighed it to the ground; it lies in the dust and bears the whole burden. The races of men [and women] with their religious factions have torn the word to pieces; they have killed for it and died for it, and it bears their fingermarks and their blood.... They draw caricatures and write "God" underneath; they murder one another to say "in God's name".... We must esteem those who interdict it because they rebel against the injustice and wrong which are so readily referred to "God" for authorization.[14]

From time immemorial, people have tried to possess God, to put God on their side and to manipulate the Divine for selfish and violent purposes.

[12] See Ellul, *Violence*, p. 130.

[13] Ellul, *Violence*, p. 130. In fact, Ellul states that "violence is contrary to the life in Christ to which we are called. Therefore, as Christians, we must firmly refuse to accept whatever justifications of violence are advanced; and in particular we must reject all attempts to justify violence on Christian ground" (*Violence*, pp. 139-140).

[14] Martin Buber, *Meetings*, La Salle: Open Court Pub. Co., 1973, pp. 50-51. As cited in Walter Kasper, *The God of Jesus Christ* (M. J. O'Connell, trans.), New York: Crossroad, 1984, pp. 3-4; see also Ramón Martínez de Pisón, *Dieu est unique mais non solitaire: Vie trinitaire et transformation humaine*, Montréal, Médiaspaul (Brèches Théologiques, 43), 2008, pp. 7-17.

This tendency can be seen in the crusade of Osama bin Laden, and of his followers, against the Western world, particularly against the United States and its allies, in the conflict between Israel and Palestine, and in the fratricidal war between Christians and Muslim in the former Yugoslavia.[15]

These manipulations of the Divine project the image of a "warrior" and "pathological God," of which we spoke in the last chapter. This portrait of God has undermined the credibility of Judaism, Christianity, and Islam. Lee Griffith observes:

> The preaching of many churches has lent greater credibility to an image of a God who intervenes in history through warfare rather than a God who intervenes in history through resurrection and the renunciation of death. As if God were somehow prone to mighty swings of mood, the terror of God has been segregated from the love of God, and the terror of God has been vested with greater credibility.[16]

In fact, Ilona N. Rashkow underlines how the image of a warrior God has served, and continues to serve, as a justification for "the holy war ideology of all three of the major religions that have their roots in the Hebrew Bible: Judaism, Christianity, and Islam. Moreover, the medieval development of 'Just War Theory,' which still shapes the philosophy and psychology of the Western nations, can be traced to this violent biblical base."[17] Mark Juergensmeyer says: "In spiritualizing violence, therefore, religion gives the resources of violence a remarkable power."[18] But this is a distortion of God's name.

Similar to the way in which Osama bin Laden wrongfully used the name of God in his crusade against the Western world, former President George W. Bush has used God's name to justify his invasion of Iraq in 2003. This invasion was part of his own crusade against evil after, and in response to, the terrorist attacks perpetrated by Al-Qaeda on the Twin Towers of the World Trade Center and the Pentagon.[19]

[15] See Jean Guy Nadeau, "Mondialisation, violence et religion: Des pratiques et discours troubles," in Noël (Ed.), *Mondialisation, violence et religion*, pp. 8-9.

[16] Griffith, *The War on Terrorism and the Terror of God*, pp. xii-xiii.

[17] Ilona N. Rashkow, "Hell Hath No Fury: God, Language, and Lacan," in Ellens (Ed.), *The Destructive Power of Religion*, vol. 2, p. 173. The "Just War Theory" was developed, in particular, by Saint Augustine. He was the first to establish the conditions justifying its use.

[18] Juergensmeyer, "Religious Terror and Global War," in Rennie and Tite (Eds.), *Religion, Terror and Violence*, p. 131. He adds, on the same page: "Ironically, the reverse is also true: terrorism can give religion power."

[19] See Michael Northcott, *An Angel Directs the Storm: Apocalyptic Religion and American Empire*, London (UK): SCM Press, 2007, pp. 31-35, 103-112, 140-141.

With both Osama bin Laden and George W. Bush there was a manipulative use of God's name. Clinton Bennett writes: "If, as I shall argue, it is not religion per se but a manipulation of religion that supports violence, its demise will not solve conflicts as long as other issues remain unresolved, such as power and wealth distribution but its manipulation towards peace may help to resolve conflict."[20] For this reason, bin Laden and Bush, among many others, can be characterized as personifying "the Redeemer complex."[21]

Griffith warns against those who view themselves as the instruments of God's terror.[22] Osama bin Laden and George W. Bush not only considered themselves the defenders of good against evil but also saw themselves as inspired and chosen by God. They both espoused a very narrow vision of the Muslim and Christian faiths. In relationship to these narrow visions, Jamal Kharder asks:

> Did God choose the faithful of any religion to announce their faith and knowledge of God by killing the other children of God? These nations should see what has led them to religious wars: Is it really for the glory of God or for the glory of humankind and their personal interests? This is the reality we are living today. We believe in God, and we reject those who have a faith different than ours.[23]

[20] Clinton Bennett *In Search of Solutions: The Problem of Religion and Conflict*, London (UK), Oakville: Equinox Publishing Ltd. (Religion and Violence), 2008, p. 11.

[21] It is important to read what Lisa Isherwood says regarding the reality we refer to with my term, "Redeemer complex," even if she does not use it herself: "We do not have to go as far back as the Crusades to be reminded of the link between religion and violence or to realize that people have always viewed that link quite differently. George W. Bush we are reminded was told by God to invade Iraq and despite the rhetoric around the action, that of salvation and redemption, we continue to be faced with the stark reality of that action–death and suffering on a scale that we will probably not fully know until many years from now when it is deemed politically alright to tell the truth. There are those in the Muslim world who saw the bringing down of the Twin Towers as a religious act, one aimed at making a brutal point about the realities of western capitalism and its own brutal/genocidal regime. The circle seems endless and the way in which we view things is quite obviously dictated by where we reside on that ever spinning wheel" ("Introduction," in Lisa Isherwood and Rosemary Radford Ruether [Eds.], *Weep Not for Your Children: Essays on Religion and Violence*, London [UK], Oakville: Equinox Publishing Ltd., 2008, p. 1).

[22] See Griffith, *The War on Terrorism and the Terror of God*, p. xiii. In the same sense, John J. Collins says: "The Bible not only witnesses to the innocent victim and to the God of victims, but also to the hungry God who devours victims and to the zeal of his human agents" ("The Zeal of Phinehas, the Bible, and the Legitimation of Violence," in Ellens [Ed.], *The Destructive Power of Religion*, vol. 1, p. 25).

[23] Jamal Kharder, "Opportunities and Threats for Religions in Conflict and Violence: How (Not) to Use the Name of God," in Jacques Haers, Norbert Hintersteiner and Georges De Schrijver (Eds.), *Postcolonial Europe in the Crucible of Cultures: Reckoning with God in a World of Conflicts*, Amsterdam, New York: Rodopi (Currents of Encounter, 34), 2007, p. 141.

The issue that Khader's questions raise is not simply the critiquing of Osama bin Laden and George W. Bush for having wrongfully used the name of God. His questions also point to dangers surrounding a nation's belief, such as that espoused by the United States, which sees itself as "God's chosen people." As Eric O. Hanson notes:

> The French philosopher Rousseau, not friend of institutional religion, first employed the term "civil religion" to name those religious sentiments such as the existence of God, personal immortality, and the sanctity of obedience to national laws that would support social order. In the American case, this cultural nationalism drew its themes from the dominant Protestant ethos: Americans are God's Chosen People, whose manifest destiny is to settle the new wilderness continent and thereby produce a righteous republic as a living sign of God's Providence for the nation and the world.[24]

Being "the bearers of God's gift (freedom)" to the world means that Americans must fight against evil, particularly evil as it is incarnated in terrorism and by their enemies. However, according to Sharon Erickson Nepstad,

> [w]hen religiosity is mixed into the process of constructing an enemy, it can intensify the conflict. If people believe that they are carrying out a divine mandate, they may be less willing to negotiate, since the devout will not compromise the will of God. Furthermore, earthly struggles may take on cosmic significance, reflecting a transcendent battle between good and evil. This type of worldview often leads people to draw rigid, impermeable divisions between groups. Evil is no longer an individual trait but rather a characteristic of an entire group that is considered incapable of change.... The only way to completely

[24] Eric O. Hanson, *Religion and Politics in the International System Today*, New York: Cambridge University Press, 2006, p. 51; see also Paul Christopher Johnson, "Savage Civil Religion," in Rennie and Tite (Eds.), *Religion, Terror and Violence*, pp. 41-65. For her part, Caryn D. Riswold criticizes as "unsatisfactory" the instrumentalisation of religion by George W. Bush after September 11, 2001, and particularly his "either with us or against us" duality (good against evil) of his "war against terrorism." She asks herself: "Problems begin to emerge when considering basic questions: Is it that easy? Can evil be defeated? Is the President of the United States God's chosen savior? Is it really certain that we, the good free Americans, are going to win?" ("The Rhetoric of Evil and Eradicating Terrorism," in Renni and Tite [Eds.], *Religion, Terror and Violence*, p. 68). Then, she adds: "These remarks inextricably link the privilege of American freedom to the will of God and place the United States in the position of the bearer of God's gift (freedom) to the rest of the world. The proposal is something like this: We have it. God gave it to us, everyone deserves it, our war against this dictator is therefore the intention of God and, so we know that God is on our side. The logic of this rhetoric is seductive, but is it appropriate? In assuming the favor of God, it implies that whatever military activity in which the country engages is thereby sanctioned by God" (p. 69; see also Northcott, *An Angel Directs the Storm*, pp. 3-13; Guy Côté, "Le messianisme politico-religieux," in *Relations*, 744 [2010], pp. 25-26).

> eliminate evil, therefore, is to annihilate the wicked and any means used to accomplish this are morally justified.[25]

Believing one has a "divine mandate" to save the world, particularly against terrorism, is one of the false moral reasons that justify the United States' use of "proactive or preemptive defense." The question is whether this perception of having a divine mandate legitimately sanctions the use of violence in response to violence. In a few Western countries, such as in the United States, religion and its manipulation are used in just this way. There is neither a presidential address, nor a political speech that does not now end with the famous expression: "God bless you! God bless the United States of America!"

3. A Morally Justified Counter-Violence?

There is no doubt that people and nations have the right to defend themselves against aggression. It is not my intention with the following argument to justify, in any way, terrorist attacks that destroy innocent lives, attempt to destroy a country's infrastructure, the physical and cultural memories of people, and the environment. What matters here is questioning violent reactions that are not so far removed from, and in a way are similar to, the violence they try to eradicate. As J. Harold Ellens points out, so-called "proactive or preemptive defense" and/or "retaliation" belong to the "law of the jungle [*Lex Talionis*]." Such types of responses as these are even more self-contradictory when we take into account that we belong to "the twenty-first century, in this supposedly civilized Western world."[26]

As soon as violence is used, it becomes very hard to draw a clear line between a "just war" and "terrorism." Griffith states that "[o]nce one justifies the use of violence, one should not be surprised to find that the line between just warrior and terrorist can be very fine indeed–fine to the point of subjectivity, fine to the point of apparition."[27] Furthermore, this proactive or preemptive violence, or the counter-violence of retaliation, is usually accompanied by the demonization of the enemies which, as

[25] Sharon Erickson Nepstad, "Religion, Violence, and Peacemaking," in *Journal for the Scientific Study of Religion*, 43/3 (2004), p. 298.

[26] J. Harold Ellens, "Religious Metaphors Can Kill," in Ellens (Ed.), *The Destructive Power of Religion*, vol. 1, pp. 255-256.

[27] Griffith, *The War on Terrorism and the Terror of God*, p. 19.

previously discussed, in turn appears to justify the use of violent actions against them.

The typical example of a reason why one should question the morality of the former President George W. Bush's "proactive or preemptive defense" against the "axis of evil" is the invasion of Iraq. This was a war without any legitimacy; the arguments for it were founded on lies.[28] In fact, today it is evident that the real reasons for this invasion were economics and the political control of the region, though hidden under the myth of "national security" policy.[29]

Despite recognizing the legality of the "Iraq-Kuwait War" or "Persian Gulf War [I]" in response to the invasion of Kuwait by Saddam Hussein (starting on August 2, 1990 and ending, with the victory of the allies, on February 28, 1991), Alan Storkey questions the "morality" of this "Gulf War I," in which victory was obtained at such a huge cost in innocent human lives: "[T]hey [the allies] finished up killing over one hundred thousand Iraqis. How right [moral] is that?"[30] What Storkey highlights is the important difference to be made between "legality" and "morality." In North American society, there is a tendency to confuse the two. Thus, for many people, what is "legal," that is to say, defined as legitimate, as what is right according to the law, is also "moral," namely, considered the correct way of behaving by more acceptable "transcendent" principles. However, something can be "legal" and not "moral." I think that this distinction can and should be applied to every war!

To appeal to Christian faith to justify proactive or preemptive defense and/or counter-violence is to "pass by" the message of Jesus Christ. According to Simon John De Vries,

> Jesus declared that the Pentateuchal rule [*Lex Talionis*] is superseded and inappropriate within his new kingdom and urged his followers to substitute kindness and generosity in the place of retaliation (Matt. 5:38-42). Jesus was not so much a revolutionary as a creative adapter and extender of biblical law. He was himself, alas, the victim of an excessive and drastic travesty of justice, less that of the book of Moses than one imposed under a harsh and cruel foreign power, the Roman Empire. It takes greater courage and determination to live by the rule he proposed than by the misdirection of political power under which he suffered.[31]

[28] See Griffith, *The War on Terrorism and the Terror of God*, p. 88.

[29] See Wink, "The Myth of Redemptive Violence," in Ellens (Ed.), *The Destructive Power of Religion*, vol. 3, pp. 278-284.

[30] Storkey, *Jesus and Politics*, p. 157.

[31] Simon John De Vries, "Scenes of Sex and Violence in the Old Testament," in Ellens (Ed.), *The Destructive Power of Religion*, vol. 1, p. 86.

In this sense, according to Walter Wink, there is a difference between "active nonviolence" and "passive nonresistance." Active nonviolence is a kind of "third way" between passive nonresistance and violent reaction.[32] This "third way" is the most reasonable one, and the only one that can stop the spiral of violence.

* * *

When violence becomes the dominant religion, it is difficult to recognize it for what it really is: a destructive force. At the same time, it is difficult to recognize the spiral of violence entered into where this false religion serves as moral justification to behave violently. In such circumstances, violence seemingly acquires a redemptive value. But this is one of the most flagrant manipulations of God, which goes against the commandment forbidding us to wrongfully use the name of God. It is in the very fullest sense a way of taking God's name in vain.

For this reason, a second conclusion to be drawn concerning the relationship between religion and violence is the need to confront "the myth of redemptive violence" and its accompanying ideas that God is on "our side" and that violent behavior is justified.[33] God cannot be domesticated or possessed. Yahweh, Jesus Christ, and Allah cannot be treated as if they were private objects. Nor can believers of the monotheistic faiths claim to know the absolute truth about the Divine. As Clinton Bennett states, the "[u]se of religious rhetoric to justify or to fuel violence is contrary to the higher principle [the principle of peace] that is embedded in scripture itself, and so is bad religion."[34] Thus, the

[32] See Walter Wink, "Can Love Save the World?," in Rennie and Tite (Eds.), *Religion, Terror and Violence*, p. 115. As Samuel M. Powell points out, discussing the position of Walter Wink, "[t]he alternative that Wink proposes is that we see Jesus as commanding an active (although nonviolent) resistance to evil. Evil, then, is not something to be tolerated but is instead something to be overcome and eliminated. Wink thus argues that the gospels show us how to respond constructively to terror and violence in a way that break the cycle of retaliation" ("Discussion: theological Reflections," in Rennie and Tite [Eds.], *Religion, Terror and Violence*, p. 123).

[33] See Wink, "The Myth of Redemptive Violence," in Ellens (Ed.), *The Destructive Power of Religion*, vol. 3, pp. 284-285.

[34] Bennett, *In Search of Solutions*, p. 213; see also Major Richard Saint-Louis, "In God We Trust," in *Prêtre et Pasteur*, 111/7 (2010), pp. 417-424. Anna S. King underlines the importance of "religious rhetoric" in retaliation: "This entire section therefore vividly warns us of the power of religious rhetoric to persuade with its oversimplified characterization of the battle of good against evil to the acceptance of inevitably violent responses to the catastrophic occurrences of 9/11. By its use of popular slogans and vivid images, and by tying its worldview to superficial evocations of Christian belief, such

religious justification of proactive or preemptive defense and/or counter-violence is often the result of "a government's rhetoric to support a political policy of violence."[35]

Contrary to these attitudes, there is a growing awareness among believers of the need to welcome the God who comes to "all of us" in abundance: "Listen! I am standing at the door, knocking; if you hear my voice and open the door, I will come in to you and eat with you, and you with me" (Rev 3:20). The Divine presence is offered to every human being, but it is not something that can be possessed, dominated or controlled, as Jesus Christ says to Nicodemus: "The wind blows where it chooses, and you hear the sound of it, but you do not know where it comes from or where it goes. So it is with everyone who is born of the Spirit" (Jn 3:8).

Indeed, the God of Abraham, of Isaac, of Jacob, of Jesus Christ, of the prophet Muhammad is, in a particular way, present in the victims of violence. Besides being morally questionable, violence is always destructive, as we will now discuss in the next chapter.

rhetoric allows no space for the exploration of alternative perspectives nor for the acknowledgment of the complexities of Islamic thought. This is not just a caution against the beguiling power of unexamined language, but also a warning that when this is itself tied to the authority and persuasiveness of state power, it can mislead us into accepting paths that will entail unpredictable and unpalatable consequences" ("Discussion: Rhetorical Reflections," in Rennie and Tite [Eds.], *Terror and Violence*, p. 100).

[35] Philip L. Tite, "Sacred Violence and the Scholar of Religion as Public Intellectual," in Rennie and Tite (Eds.), *Religion, Terror and Violence*, p. 5.

Chapter 3

Consequences of Violence

To speak of violence is to recognize the existence of those who suffer its consequences. For victims, the scars of violence can remain forever. In this chapter, I address the effects of violence inflicted on innocent victims, recognizing that one of the consequences of violence is also to effect or give rise to further perpetrators of violence. I will examine this last dimension of violence in Chapter 4 below.

Violence produces an erosion of human dignity, community cohesion, and culture, as I argue in the first part of this chapter. As a result of violence, victims feel deeply diminished in their own integrity and dignity. A similar diminishment occurs in community wholeness and in people's ability to respect other cultures. But, as I stress in the second part, children, adolescents, aboriginal peoples, the LGBTQ community, and women are often the most vulnerable victims of violence. Finally, in the third part, I focus on the "ecological holocaust," that is, on the violence inflicted upon the environment.

1. Erosion of Human Dignity, Community Cohesion, and Culture

As Maurice Bellet indicates, violence can be defined as the absence and death of relationships, because it destroys the humanity of both the person who suffers violence and its perpetrator.[1] The erosion of human dignity and personal integrity are some of the most tragic forms of violence.[2] Oftentimes, the humiliation inflicted upon the victims is so overwhelming that some of them attempt to, or even succeed in, committing suicide. When a person or a nation feels humiliated, that humiliation can become a particularly acute source of shame. As I discuss in the next chapter below, humiliation and shame can serve as a trigger for entering into a spiral of violence in that they become the source of continuing cycles of violence.

[1] See Bellet, *"Je ne suis pas venu apporter la paix..."*, pp. 30-33.
[2] See Bellet, *"Je ne suis pas venu apporter la paix..."*, pp. 25-26.

Humiliation and its resultant shame have become weapons of war. Through violence, perpetrators humiliate and shame their victims to destroy their self-esteem. Primo Levi, a holocaust survivor witnesses to the fact that, and the way in which, human dignity is eroded in times of war. In these circumstances, victims of atrocities can fall to the same level of brutality as those who are brutalizing them. In a very strong statement, he describes the "collaborators" in Nazi concentration camps:

> But collaborators, who originate in the adversary camp, ex-enemies, are untrustworthy by definition: they betrayed once and they can betray again. It is not enough to relegate them to marginal tasks; the best way to bind them is to burden them with guilt, cover them with blood, compromise them as much as possible, thus establishing a bond of complicity so that they can no longer turn back. This way of proceeding has been well known to criminal associations of all times and places.[3]

As Levi's quotation underscores, one of the consequences of the erosion of human dignity is what Donald E. Sloat calls "spiritual abuse." For Sloat, this abuse is comparable to a "terrorism of the soul."[4] Christians, for example, were accustomed to the so-called "pastoral practice of fear." Church authorities, theologians and preachers used fear as a way of making people behave according to the norms and morality presented to them by the official teaching of the Church. This "pastoral" approach existed long before the Protestant Reformation in the sixteenth century, and has continued in both Reformed and Roman Catholic traditions. The use of fear, particularly of eternal damnation, to motivate people and, one could say, manipulate consciences, was a regular practice in many Christian churches until recently.

Relationships, here understood as constituting the very heart of the community, are also affected by violence. Lee Griffith writes:

> Massacre on a massive scale is not a sign of age-old hatreds that have prevented community formation; it is a sign of new hatreds that have been generated intentionally to disrupt and destroy communities that already existed. Why? Because strong, pluralistic communities consti-

[3] Primo Levi, "The Gray Zone," in Nancy Scherper-Hughes and Philippe Bourgois (Eds.), *Violence in War and Peace: An Anthology*, Malden: Blackwell Publishing, 2004, p. 85. A few pages later, Levi says: "Compassion and brutality can coexist in the same individual and in the same moment, despite all logic; and for all that, compassion itself eludes logic" (p. 90).

[4] See Donald E. Sloat, "Terrorizing the Self to Save the Soul: The Destructive Power of Legalistic Christianity," in Ellens (Ed.), *The Destructive Power of Religion*, vol. 3, pp. 151-174.

> tute a threat to the unhindered exercise of political and military power. Terror can be both reflective of community disintegration and a means of fostering further disintegration by leaving people feeling unsafe, suspicious, and disconnected. Grotesques acts of terrorism that entail the dismemberment of human bodies and sometimes used to communicate the message that the community itself is being dismembered.[5]

In instances of extreme violence such as terrorism, the Latin maxim, "divide et impera" ("divide and rule" or "divide and conquer"), becomes a reality. Here, terrorism is used to destroy the bonds of the community in order to control and/or to dominate its members. The disintegration of the community's cohesion brings people to a kind of total isolation. It is in these circumstances that the community can be easily manipulated.

Together with individuals and communities, violence also affects culture. Speaking of his own experience as a war journalist, Chris Hedges has often stated that

> [t]he destruction of culture in wartime is also physical. There is an effort to eradicate the monuments and buildings that challenge the myth of the nation. There are thousands of Armenian villages in Turkey, Kurdish villages in Iraq, and Palestinian villages in Israel that have been razed in this process of state-sponsored forgetting. Along with their destruction has been a ferocious campaign to deny the displaced the right to remember where they once belonged.[6]

War, then, deforms and/or destroys the cultural identity of peoples. This happens, particularly, when a nation is formed by and made up of different cultural and religious ethnicities.[7] Thus, a group demonizes and deforms the culture and the religion of the other group in order to justify its aggression against it. This situation has perduring consequences because, as Redekop underlines, "[d]isplaced men and women carry within themselves the effects of deep-rooted conflict."[8]

This is one of the reasons why the psychological and physical scars of violence are so difficult to overcome and, above all, why it is so hard to forgive. Not only has it become difficult to forgive the perpetrators of violence but also to forgive oneself for having endured so much humiliation. There exist particular groups of persons, however, who are more affected by violence than others.

[5] Griffith, *The War on Terrorism and the Terror of God*, pp. 46-47.
[6] Hedges, *War Is a Force that Gives Us Meaning*, p. 72.
[7] See Redekop, *From Violence to Blessing*, p. 11.
[8] Redekop, *From Violence to Blessing*, p. 22.

2. Children, Adolescents, Aboriginal Peoples, the LGBTQ Community, and Women

Violence against children, adolescents, aboriginal peoples, the LGBTQ community, and women has assumed alarming proportions.[9] Psychological, physical and, especially, sexual violence inflicted on them reveals a terrifying dimension of contemporary society that raises urgent questions about the long-term repercussions of such violence.[10] The sexual commerce of children and adolescents in underdeveloped countries, catering to Westerners, ought to make people cry out to heaven.[11] Regrettably, sexual violence committed against the poorest and most vulnerable people in society is only one of the many manifestations of the violence that affects children and adolescents. They are also often used as child soldiers and as slave labor in countries around the world.[12]

In the United States and Canada, as in many European countries, one of the worst forms of violence inflicted upon children, adolescents, and aboriginal peoples, is sexual abuse by members of the clergy and of

[9] See Bellet, *"Je ne suis pas venu apporter la paix..."*, p. 37; Penni Stewart, "Orientation, Gender Identity Deserve Protection," in *CAUT/ACPPU Bulletin*, 58/2 (2011), p. A3. In my research, I have not included a consideration of "elder abuse," which has received less attention until recently. However, elder women are the most vulnerable targets. Anne V. Gormly and David M. Brodzinsky say in this regard: "Although abuse of elderly has been reported within public and private institutions, more often than not the elderly are abused by a member of their own family. Furthermore, elder abuse is far less likely than child abuse to be reported to authorities.... Ageist attitudes may also help to contribute to psychological and financial abuse and the violation of basic rights of the elderly. Sometimes adult children view their aging parents as incapable of making any of their own decisions because they are old, and they take over all decision making without consulting with or securing the consent of their parents" (*Lifespan Human Development* [5th ed.], Forth Worth: Harcourt Brace College Publishers, 1993 [© 1979], p. 587).

[10] See Gayle Rubin, "The Traffic in Women: Notes on the Political Economy of Sex," in Rayna R. Reither (Ed.), *Toward an Anthropology of Women*, New York: Monthly Review Press, 1975, pp. 157-210; Margarita Todorova, "Prostitution and the Church's Task with Reference to Bulgaria," in *Feminist Theology*, 20 (1999), pp. 29-37.

[11] See Ramón Martínez de Pisón, *Sin and Evil* (R. R. Cooper, trans.), Sherbrooke: Médiaspaul, 2002, pp. 96-105.

[12] See "Military Use of Children," at http://en.wikipedia.org/wiki/Military_use_of_children (accessed September 28, 2011); *Le martyre des innocents: L'exploitation du travail des enfants en Inde, à la recherche des causes fondamentales*, in *Droit de la personne: Bulletin d'information sur la recherche et l'enseignement*, 32 (1996), the whole thematic issue; Thaksina Khaikaew, "Doctors Travail to Thailand's Remote Regions Bearing New Smiles: Poverty Has Made Facial Disfigurement All Too Common among Children. Surgeons Are Coming to their Rescue Free of Charge," in *The Globe and Mail*, Saturday, February 20, 1999, p. A7D; Kohn Pomfret, "North Koreans Sell Daughters for Food," in *Guardian Weekly*, Sunday, February 28, 1999, p. 17.

religious congregations. As Oliver J. McTernan highlights, "I want to acknowledge… the seriousness of the violence suffered in God's name by the victims of… the child sexual abuse that seems to have thrived for several decades under a clerical culture of denial within the Catholic Church."[13] The official apology on behalf of the Canadian Government offered by Prime Minister, Stephen Harper, on June 11, 2008, to former aboriginal students of residential schools, their families and communities, for the physical, sexual and cultural violence inflicted by school personnel and especially by members of religious congregations, is an example of the need to acknowledge the facts of what actually happened to these children. As I point out in Chapter 6 below, this acknowledgement is necessary if one is to enter into the "difficult" process of forgiveness and reconciliation.

For his part, Pope Benedict XVI wrote a *Pastoral Letter to the Catholics of Ireland* (on March 19, 2010), asking the Irish victims of sexual abuse by the members of the clergy and religious congregations for forgiveness in the name of the Roman Catholic Church. He asked victims to forgive so many years of sexual abuse by many of those who had spoken to them about God's love and apologized for the denial and/or cover-up of the problem by Church authorities.[14] The Pope has done the same, if in a less official way, in other parts of the world. The plague of sexual abuse of minors by members of the clergy and religious congregations haunts Benedict XVI wherever he goes!

Among the various forms of violence inflicted on particular groups in society, there is a need to acknowledge homophobic attitudes and violence perpetrated against the LGBTQ community. Both self-alienation and alienation from others, due to these attitudes and other forms of

[13] McTernan, *Violence in God's Name*, p. xvi; see also pp. 153-154; Hanson, *Religion and Politics in the International System Today*, pp. 132-133; "Trauma & Transformation: The Catholic Church and the Sexual Abuse Crisis," at http://traumaandtransformation.org/the-conference (accessed October 17, 2011). Jean Guy Nadeau and Sheila A. Redmond speak of the deformed idea of God those children, victims of sexual abuse, develop when they realize that God, supposedly a protector of innocents, does not intervene in stopping the abuse. This is even more tragic when violence is inflicted upon them by religious leaders (see "Le Dieu des victims reconsidéré à partir des victims d'abus sexuels durant l'enfance," in Noël [Ed.], *Mondialisation, violence et religion*, pp. 122-123).

[14] See Benedict XVI, *Pastoral Letter to the Catholics of Ireland*, at http://www.vatican.va/holy_father/benedict_xvi/letters/2010/documents/hf_ben-xvi_let_20100319_church-ireland_en.html (accessed September 29, 2011); see also "Toward Healing and Renewal: A Symposium for Catholic Bishops and Religious Superiors on Sexual Abuse of Minors," Pontifical Gregorian University, Rome, February 6-9, 2012, at http://thr.unigre.it/vescovi2012/en-gb/presspublic/press/documents.aspx (accessed February 10, 2012).

violence, are present in these groups and can lead to suicide or at least attempts at suicide.[15] As Annette Beautrais emphasizes, "[s]pecifically, it has been argued that, because of a series of social processes centering around homophobic attitudes, gay, lesbian and bisexual youth are exposed to serious social and personal stresses that increase their likelihood of suicidal behavior."[16] From what I have seen, I can personally corroborate what she says regarding this last point. During my years growing up in Jaén, a town in Andalusia (South of Spain), I saw how my culture of origin, along with many others, reflected homophobic attitudes. Those who were lesbian, gay, bisexual, and queer had to live in social isolation, ashamed, stigmatized, and prone to suicide. They questioned their own sexual orientation and, as a result, frequently became alienated from their own selves. What is still more difficult to understand is the negative attitude that generally persisted among the three monotheistic religions toward the LGBTQ community.[17]

Violence against women is well documented throughout history.[18] What is more, it is neither a characteristic of any particular social class, nor of any culture or religion.[19] It is a phenomenon which crosses almost

[15] See Martínez de Pisón, *Death by Despair*, pp. 26-28; Stewart, "Orientation, Gender Identity Deserve Protection," p. A3.

[16] Annette Beautrais, "Risk Factors for Suicide and Attempted Suicide among Young People," in *Australian and New Zealand Journal of Psychiatry*, 34/3 (2000), p. 424.

[17] See Isherwood, "Introduction," in Lisa Isherwood and Rosemary Radford Ruether (Eds.), *Weep Not for Your Children*, pp. 2-4. Marc Juergensmeyer makes a good point regarding homophobic attitudes of "religious activists": "Why," he asks, "have such aversions to homosexuality been held so strongly by contemporary religious activists? One answer is a loss of identity: the kind of heterosexual male who is attracted to such movements is precisely the sort who loses power in a society in which women and gays have access to straight males' traditional positions of authority. They see women and gays as competition.

"But there is another answer to the question of why radical religious groups are so homophobic: a loss of control.... When men have perceived their roles as diminished in a socio-economic system that denies a sense of agency to individuals, either by being incompetent or overly competent–a faceless mechanical bureaucracy–this challenge has led to a defense of traditional roles. Because men have so frequently held the reins of public order as their gendered responsibility in society in the past, they have felt particularly vulnerable when the public world has fallen apart or has seemed beyond control. In this case, they have seen active women and gays not just as competition, but as symptoms of a world gone awry" (*Terror in the Mind of God*, pp. 200-201).

[18] See *Violence against Women*, in *Concilium*, 1 (1994), the whole thematic issue.

[19] See "Comité des affaires sociales de l'Assemblée des évêques du Québec," *Violence en héritage?: Réflexion pastorale sur la violence conjugale*, Montréal: Assemblée des évêques du Québec, 1989, pp. 28-29 (from now on cited *Violence en héritage?*); Victoria Rollins, "The Power of Male Violence as Evil: Uses and Abuses of Power in the Shoah and the Silent Genocide of Abused Women," in Isherwood and Ruether (Eds.), *Weep Not For Your Children*, pp. 187-213.

all socially constructed boundaries.[20] Patriarchal cultures have conveyed a dominant relationship of male over female that has not completely vanished in our times. Strong indications of this bias against women can be seen when feminism is compared by some men to an ideology such as Nazism.[21] This prejudice is also reflected in the words of Judge Denys Dionne, spoken during a trial in 1989 (in Longueil, Quebec): "Rules are like a woman, they are made to be violated."[22] Again, this chauvinism is physically manifested when women continue to be systematically raped as a "weapon of war" or killed in the name of "honor,"[23] or when they are used as objects, traded for sexual purposes into prostitution and/or pornography.[24] Unfortunately, religious traditions are not blameless.[25] In spite of the numerous proclamations of the equality of men and women made by Christian churches,[26] such words often remain mere rhetoric in practice. The inequality is realized and celebrated ritually as women are barred from ordination[27] and other forms of leadership within the Roman Catholic Church,[28] or when looking at the whole reaction provoked by

[20] See Nancy Nason-Clark, "When Terror Strikes at Home: The Interface between Religion and Domestic Violence," in *Journal for the Scientific Study of Religion*, 43/3 (2004), p. 308.

[21] See David Shackleton, "Feminism Exposed: Our Blindness to Feminine Evils," in *Everyman: A Men's Journal*, 35 (1999), pp. 4-6, 46-50.

[22] Cited by Sandra Martin, "Stupid Judge Tricks," in *The Globe and Mail*, Saturday, March 13, 1999 (at http://www.fact.on.ca/newpaper/gm99031d.htm [accessed September 28, 2011]).

[23] See Veerle Draulans, "Human Dignity Violated by Increasing Aggression: A Gender Analysis," in Haers, Hintersteiner and Schrijver (Eds.), *Postcolonial Europe in the Crucible of Cultures*, pp. 235-236; Nicole Soleto, "The Hidden Wars: Violence against Women and Just War Theory," in Isherwood and Ruether (Eds.), *Weep Not For Your Children*, pp. 90-111; Marianne Kamp, "Femicide as Terrorism: The Case of Uzbekistan's Unveiling Murders," in James K. Wellman, Jr. (Ed.), *Belief and Bloodshed: Religion and Violence across Time and Tradition*, Lanham: Rowman & Littlefield Publishers, Inc., 2007, pp. 131-132.

[24] See Monique Dumais, "Voies de salut pour les femmes dans le contexte de la violence mondialisée," in Noël (Ed.), *Mondialisation, violence et religion*, pp. 79-80.

[25] See *Dossier: Pourquoi fait-elle si peur?: La femme dans les religions*, in *Le Monde des Religions*, 33 (2009), pp. 20-47.

[26] See, for example, John Paul II, *Apostolic Letter* Mulieris Dignitatem *on the Dignity and Vocation of Women on the Occasion of the Marian Year*, at http://www.vatican.va/holy_father/john_paul_ii/apost_letters/documents/hf_jp-ii_apl_15081988_mulieris-dignitatem_en.html (accessed September 29, 2011).

[27] See John Paul II, *Apostolic Letter* Ordinatio Sacerdotalis *on Reserving Priestly Ordination to Men* [*sic*] *Alone*, at http://www.vatican.va/holy_father/john_paul_ii/apost_letters/documents/hf_jp-ii_apl_22051994_ordinatio-sacerdotalis_en.html (accessed September 29, 2011).

[28] See Miriam K. Martin, "Woman and Worship: The Conversation Continues," in *Église et Théologie*, 28/3 (1997), pp. 301-317; Carmiña Navia Velasco, "Au revers de l'histoire: Les femmes," in *Relations*, 752 (2011), pp. 22-23.

the admission of women to the priesthood in the Anglican Church. A male Anglican priest reacted to the ordination of women by describing them as "bitches" that ought to be burned as witches were in the Middle Ages.[29] The question can be raised: What image of God, creation and, especially, of women, does this priest promote?

Specifically, violence against women within the family is a major problem.[30] The statistics on violence inflicted upon women within this family context in Canada and in other parts of the world are alarming.[31] Because of the alarming rate of domestic violence indicated by her research, Veerle Draulans entitles one section of her article on the violation of women's dignity within the family as follows: "The Family is Holy but not Always Safe."[32] Nevertheless, statistics alone are not sufficient to give an accurate account of the extent of violence against women in family situations. Often violence against them is not

[29] See "Anglican Vicar Calls Female Priests 'Bitches'," in *The Ottawa Citizen*, Wednesday, March 9, 1994, pp. A1, A12.

[30] The document *Violence en héritage?* defines violence against women within the family context as any kind of "psychological, verbal or physical" behavior on the part of the spouse/partner (see pp. 10-14). Such violence can be the result of individual causes as well of the environment of the violent person, and of socio-cultural, economic and structural influences such as, for example, patriarchy (see pp. 15, 28-38; see also Nancy Eileen Nienhuis, "Theological Reflections on Violence and Abuse," in *The Journal of Pastoral Care & Counseling*, 59/1-2 [2005], p. 121).

[31] See *Violence en héritage?*, p. 7. On this page, the Committee gives statistics for Canada, including the Province of Quebec. In the United States, "[d]omestic violence is still the leading reason that U.S. women visit emergency rooms.... Quite simply, violence against women is an epidemic" (Nienhuis, "Theological Reflections on Violence and Abuse," p. 110). More recently, in 2007, according to some sources, "at least six women die every month in France as a result of injuries caused by their male partners.... One out of ten women in France finds her own home to be the most deadful place to live" (Draulans, "Human Dignity Violated by Increasing Aggression," in Haers, Hintersteiner and Schrijver [Eds.], *Postcolonial Europe in the Crucible of Cultures*, p. 240). As stated by Draulans, partner violence is as much a cause of death as cancer for women between 15 and 44. In fact, what is surprising is the young age of women already battered by their male partners: in France, women between the ages of 20 and 24 suffer more partner violence than older women. This shows how, in spite of the laws against domestic violence, campaigns of sensitization against it, and so on, young male partners continue to be a source of violence in marital/partner relationships (see Draulans, "Human Dignity Violated by Increasing Aggression," in Haers, Hintersteiner and Schrijver [Eds.], *Postcolonial Europe in the Crucible of Cultures*, pp. 240-242). Unfortunately, these statistics have not changed substantially in our present reality, as can be seen by doing a simple Google search on "women and violence."

[32] See Draulans, "Human Dignity Violated by Increasing Aggression," in Haers, Hintersteiner and Schrijver (Eds.), *Postcolonial Europe in the Crucible of Cultures*, pp. 243-244.

documented, due to socio-cultural and religious taboos about family privacy. As Sophie Chirongoma affirms regarding Zimbabwe, a geographical and cultural milieu quite different from that of the West, "[w]omen have come to internalize violence as the norm and many of them believe that husbands are justified in beating wives who refuse to have sex with them. Culture calls for women to be silent about their pain, especially if speaking out will reveal the bad secrets of the family."[33] What Chirongoma says concerning the situation of women in Zimbabwe is also common enough in Western countries. There is a rule within dysfunctional families that people, particularly women, are forbidden from speaking out about these abusive, and often lethal, situations: "You do not speak out about bad things happening within the family." For this reason, if a woman speaks out, she risks feeling guilty, besides being considered as a traitor to the family and its secret life by other members of the family and particularly by the abusive spouse/partner. Consequently, not only do women suffer in silence but they also become co-dependent in the violence perpetrated against them. This, in turn, perpetuates the spiral of abuse. As Draulans states, "[m]ost often the victims as well as the neighborhood know about the occurrence of partner violence, but they are usually silent about it. Many people see such form of violence as a private affair that does not require any interference–and certainly not legal interference."[34]

To speak of domestic violence against women also means to speak of violence against children who become, most often, passive witnesses to these traumatic events.[35] They become persons who are affected

[33] Sophie Chirongoma, "Women's and Children's Rights in the time of HIV and AIDS in Zimbawe: An Analysis of Gender Inequalities and its Impact on People's Health," in *Journal of Theology for Southern Africa*, 126 (2006), p. 56.

[34] Draulans, "Human Dignity Violated by Increasing Aggression," in Haers, Hintersteiner and Schrijver (Eds.), *Postcolonial Europe in the Crucible of Cultures*, p. 242; see also 245. The social taboo regarding family's privacy is also present within Christian contexts (see *Violence en héritage?*, pp. 7-13, 17). For this reason, members of Christian communities are invited to overcome the taboo of silence and to "speak out" courageously about any kind of perpetrated violence, and specifically, violence inflicted upon women in the family.

[35] It is interesting to read the experience that Nancy Eileen Nienhuis documents regarding children witnessing violence within the marriage: "Some years back," she says, "I had the occasion to eat lunch with an eight-year-old boy who was living at a Dallas-area shelter for battered women. Somehow 'Jack' and I got into a discussion of marriage. I asked him whether he thought he would ever marry. He thought for a while and then shook his head *no*. 'Why not?' I asked. Again he paused before answering–for much longer than I was used to from eight-year-old boys. Finally he said, 'There's too much hitting in marriage'" ("Theological Reflections on Violence and Abuse," p. 109).

for life and who are also at risk of becoming perpetrators themselves, perpetuating the pattern of violence against their own spouses in the future.[36]

What is still more alarming is that religion can become an additional factor in domestic violence. As Nancy Eileen Nienhuis observes, when we take into consideration the generalized religious background of women in the United States, and indeed we could say in Canada and in many other countries around the world, "[m]any a woman believes (or her spouse argues) that her religious faith entitles her husband to access her for sex anytime he wishes, even without her consent (*i.e.*, he is entitled to rape her). Her crisis is physical and emotional, certainly, but it is also often spiritual."[37] What are, then, the differences, apart from some cultural and socio-economic variations, between women in North America, in Europe, and those of Zimbabwe described by Chirongoma? In each context, the fact remains that adult women live with a greater probability of experiencing violence in families.

It is critical, then, that people, particularly religious leaders working with families, but also believers in general, be alerted to the lethal influence that can be exercised by persons with a distorted interpretation of some religious concepts condoning domestic violence. To add a "religious meaning" to the acceptance of violence inflicted on anyone, in this case upon women inside the family, can contribute to covering up the problem and distorting the very nature of the violent act itself.

[36] According to *Violence en héritage?*, in the province of Quebec, 50% of husbands who batter women were themselves battered as children *versus* one third of women in the same circumstances. And 52% of husbands who do the same were witnesses of violence as children *versus* 31.5% of women in the same circumstances (see p. 29).

[37] Nienhuis, "Theological Reflections on Violence and Abuse," p. 110. In this regard, she adds: "The advice women often receive from religious leaders raises some critical questions about the connections between theology and violence and abuse. How did self-sacrifice and obedience, even in the face of abuse and violence, come to be understood by some as the definition of a faithful Christian identity? I want to respond to that question by briefly tracing two relevant trajectories in theological thinking that have survived the centuries with remarkably little change: first, that suffering is sent from God, and obedience in the face of it is a sign of godliness; and, second, that women have an inferior moral nature and thus need to be under the control of men lest society find itself in chaos" (p. 111; see also Rosemary Radford Ruether, "Religion, Reproduction and Violence against Women," in Isherwood and Ruether [Eds.], *Weep Not for Your Children*, pp. 7-25; Lisa Isherwood, "The Violence of Gender: Christian Marriage as Test Case," in Isherwood and Ruether [Eds.], *Weep Not for Your Children*, pp. 54-64).

How then to eliminate an understanding of suffering that could become an additional source of distress for women already overburdened in the family milieu? As Nienhuis states clearly, "[a]ny theology that encourages us to view suffering as part of God's plan is a dangerous theology. If a battered woman acts to get out of her suffering, is she going against the will of God?"[38] Certainly not! Nienhuis goes on to say, referring to persons within a Christian context, "[i]f we encourage the belief that suffering should be accepted as a means of becoming like Christ, we are endorsing violence as a vehicle for Christian character development."[39] Yet, this is precisely the detrimental practice of the past that, in many ways, is still present today. "For centuries," Nienhuis rightly says, "a theology of suffering has operated in Christianity to encourage women to accept violence for some larger good."[40] As a result, women cannot go against God's will, and, ironically, against their well-being and salvation. As she concludes, "[o]n a larger scale, this theology ultimately leaves suffering in place–it glorifies the sufferer with a reward of heaven, but it does nothing to keep the next victim from similar abuse. In fact, it does the opposite. Thus, a Christian theological understanding of suffering requires careful considerations as we deal with violence and abuse."[41] Moreover, this inadequate understanding of suffering is very often accompanied by a false interpretation of forgiveness. Forgiveness, as I will say in Chapter 6 below, is also a fundamental dimension of the three monotheistic religious traditions and of its public role in society. However, there is a widespread agreement that forgiveness, or any other religious concept such as redemptive suffering, should not, and cannot legitimately, be used to give religious meaning or religious justification to violence.[42]

Finally, there is the violence inflicted upon creation, namely, against the environment.

[38] Nienhuis, "Theological Reflections on Violence and Abuse," p. 112.

[39] Nienhuis, "Theological Reflections on Violence and Abuse," p. 112.

[40] Nienhuis, "Theological Reflections on Violence and Abuse," p. 112.

[41] Nienhuis, "Theological Reflections on Violence and Abuse," p. 114.

[42] See Thomas Brudholm and Thomas Cushman, "Introduction: The Religious in Responses to Mass Atrocity," in Thomas Brudholm and Thomas Cushman (Eds.), *The Religious in Responses to Mass Atrocity: Interdisciplinary Perspectives*, New York: Cambridge University Press, 2009, pp. 4-5; Jennifer L. Geddes, "Religious Rhetoric in Response to Atrocity," in Brudholm and Cushman (Eds.), *The Religious in Responses to Mass Atrocity*, pp. 21, 27, 31-32; Thomas Brudholm, "On the Advocacy of Forgiveness after Mass Atrocity," in Brudholm and Cushman (Eds.), *The Religious in Responses to Mass Atrocity*, p. 143.

3. "Ecological Holocaust"

The ecological crisis of our time reveals another important dimension of the "sin of the world," to use an expression from the Gospel of John (1:29).[43] Together with the violence inflicted upon children, adolescents, aboriginal peoples, the LGBTQ community, and women, this is a sin committed by the violent behavior of human beings against the environment and the integrity of the Earth.[44] Our actions do indeed have ecological repercussions. This situation in which these repercussions are negative, here named the "ecological holocaust,"[45] is the consequence of an androcentric, patriarchal world view. The result, according to Claude Lévi-Strauss (1908–2009) and Catharina Halkes, is the "rape" and "destruction" of the soil, of mother Earth.[46] Against this worldview, there has emerged a critique of the negative role that religions, particularly Judaism, Christianity, and Islam, have played in the ecological crisis.[47] Consequently, the main conclusion to be drawn from the threat of an "ecological holocaust" is that it is not possible to hope in an ultimate future where only human beings survive. If creation perishes, if Earth is decimated, humanity goes with it.[48] For this reason, Jacques Haers highlights how "[t]oday's most crucial and urgent global threat is without a doubt the environmental challenge."[49] This is also the claim of Leonardo Boff. He connects

[43] The sin of the world refers to the sin that arises from the immoral behavior of human beings. Our actions have social, economic, political, cultural, religious and ecological repercussions as well, and not only at a personal level.

[44] See Louis Vaillancourt, "Christianisme, violence et écologie: De la défaillance assumée au défi à relever," in Noël (Ed.), *Mondialisation, violence et religion*, pp. 17-28; Jacques Racine, "Les formes de violence émergeant de la mondialisation: Une réflexion théologique," in Noël (Ed.), *Mondialisation, violence et religion*, pp. 42-44.

[45] See Hans Schwarz, *Eschatology*, Grand Rapids: William B. Eerdmans Publishing Co., 2000, pp. 194-209; Martínez de Pison, *Life beyond Death*, p. 69.

[46] See Claude Lévi-Strauss, *Tristes tropiques*, Paris: Plon (Terre Humaine), 1955, p. 103; Claude Lévi-Strauss, *L'origine des manières de table*, Paris: Plon (Mythologiques, 3), 1968, p. 422; Catharina Halkes, "The Rape of Mother Earth: Ecology and Patriarchy," in Elisabeth Schüssler Fiorenza (Ed.), *The Power of Naming: A Concilium Reader in Feminist Liberation Theology*, Maryknoll, London (UK): Orbis Books, SCM Press (Concilium Series), 1996, pp. 132-141.

[47] See Heather Eaton, "This Sacred Earth: At the Nexus of Religion, Ecology and Politics," in *Pastoral Sciences*, 23/1 (2004), pp. 35-54.

[48] See Ramón Martínez de Pisón, "Does Hope Have Meaning in the Western World?," in *Theoforum*, 36/2 (2005), pp. 175-185.

[49] Jacques Haers, "Introduction: Europe's Global Context as a Theological Challenge," in Haers, Hintersteiner and Schrijver (Eds.), *Postcolonial Europe in the Crucible of Cultures*, p. 6. The author points out how, in spite of all the efforts in recognizing the

"the cry of the oppressed with the cry of the Earth."[50] The Earth suffers the same devastating consequences as the weak and the poor of this world who are exploited by the selfish and powerful. Boff's language is very strong as he asserts that those who are the so-called "stewards" of creation have been transformed into "Earth's Satan."[51] The present situation with respect to creation has, however, made people increasingly aware of the need to establish a relationship between science and faith that is more encompassing, dialogical and less reductionist. Such a relationship is needed to recognize and reaffirm the intrinsic bond between human beings and nature.

Yet, a dualistic and Manichean vision of the world destroys the positive idea of creation and the harmony of human beings within it (see Gen 1–3).[52] Unfortunately, the results of such a vision as this are well known: human beings become predators of the environment. For this reason, as Leonardo Boff underlines, not only do the poor need to be liberated from the oppression of the selfish and powerful, but also "mother Earth" needs to be freed therefrom.[53] For him, human beings are called to contribute to the transformation of the visible world in a sacrament of Trinitarian love: creation is the body of the Trinity.[54] Boff points out how reclaiming the dignity of Earth implies as well the very reclaiming of its sacredness. This is the only way to establish a new covenant with creation.[55] At the heart of the Trinity, the central belief of Christian faith, there is solidarity, love, otherness and, particularly, connectedness. Thus, as Boff stresses,

importance of the environment, it is still very difficult to become conscious of the real threat of its destruction (see pp. 7-8).

[50] Leonardo Boff, *Cry of the Earth, Cry of the Poor* (Ph. Berryman, trans.), Maryknowll: Orbis Books, 2005 (©1997), p. xi; see also François Houtart, "Pour un nouveau rapport à la nature," in *Relations*, 752 (2011), pp. 25-27.

[51] Boff, *Cry of the Earth, Cry of the Poor*, p. xi.

[52] In this regard, Thomas Römer underlines the cultural context of the biblical authors. According to him, they "were deeply marked by the Middle East's culture and knew the great myths on the origins of the world. In these myths, the creation of the world and of the man [and woman] was the result of acts of great violence" ("De meurtres et de guerres: Le Dieu de la Bible hébraïque aime-t-il la violence?," in Marguerat [Ed.], *Dieu est-il violent?*, p. 36 [my translation]). The creation narratives of Genesis are written, precisely, as a way of overcoming dualistic and Manichean conceptions of the world (see Wink, "The Myth of Redemptive Violence," in Ellens [Ed.], *The Destructive Power of Religion*, vol. 3, pp. 266-269).

[53] See Boff, *Cry of the Earth, Cry of the Poor*, p. xii.

[54] See Leonardo Boff, *Trinité et société* (F. Malley, trans.), Paris: Éditions du Cerf (Libération, 5), 1990, p. 270-271.

[55] See Boff, *Cry of the Earth, Cry of the Poor*, p. 115.

> [t]he new paradigm that is coming to birth–that of connectedness–will be the basis of a universal religion that will only be truly universal if it seeks convergences in religious diversity. The convergences to be achieved must have to do with restoring the sacredness of all things, reclaiming the dignity of the Earth, rediscovering the mission of the human being–man and woman–called to celebrate the mystery of the cosmos, and finally, encountering God, mystery of communion and life, in the process of cosmogenesis itself.[56]

What is important is not simply addressing the violence inflicted upon the environment. It is also crucial to recognize, as Thomas F. Homer-Dixon explains, how "environmental scarcity," the result of human exploitation of the environment, also has social effects. Destroying the environment becomes a potential source of conflict and violence. This is what social scientists call "reciprocal causation."[57]

* * *

The third conclusion to be drawn from the preceding discussion refers to the importance of taking into consideration the victims of violence. Violence has become such a constant in the Western cultural imagination that we risk focusing too much on the perpetrators of violence and not enough on the victims. Contrary to the "warrior" God discussed in the first chapter above, and the domestication and manipulation of the Divine for justifying violence, as presented in the second chapter, the God of the monotheistic religions is a God of the victim. As Lee Griffith states, "[v]iolence is inevitably a renunciation rather than an affirmation of the will and freedom of God."[58] This is one of the reasons why, in

[56] Boff, *Cry of the Earth, Cry of the Poor*, p. xii. It is also interesting what Anne Primavesi says in this regard: "Without that intrinsic connection between myself and earth's self, my significant relationships with other human beings could not occur. Without it, I cease to relate to anything or anyone. This is another way of saying that my self exists because earth's self exists; and that if earth's self did not exist, the self I call mine would not exist. And that if I did not exist, earth's self would still exist. This is where the demand for geocentrism demands a change in self perspective. Priority is not something *I* can bestow on earth. Earth's self simply has, and will always have, physical, temporal and existential priority over mine" (*Gaia's Gift: Earth, Ourselves and God after Copernicus*, London [UK], New York: Routledge, 2003, p. 81; see also pp. 82-85).

[57] See Thomas F. Homer-Dixon, *Environment, Scarcity, and Violence*, Princeton: Princeton University Press, 1999, pp. 6-7. A few pages before, Homer-Dixon makes a clear presentation of how "environmental scarcity," in all of its manifestations, can be a source of violence at the national as well as at the international level (see pp. 3-4).

[58] Griffith, *The War on Terrorism and the Terror of God*, p. xiii.

Chapter 5 below, I will present a different image of God, one completely opposed to "the pathological portraits" that we have noted so far.

The violence inflicted upon children, adolescents, aboriginal peoples, the LGBTQ community, and women, is a betrayal of humanity and God's Covenant with all of creation. In this regard, as has been the case with sexual abuse, religious communities and their leaders must overcome a culture of secrecy and denial in order to arrive at a "zero tolerance" of any kind of abuse, but particularly that perpetrated upon the most vulnerable.

In a particular way, I would like to make the point regarding violence against women, because they have been considered as sub-human for millennia. The expression "women's holocaust" could be used when taking into consideration the ordeals, even death, that women have suffered in the past and in the present. My colleague, Miriam K. Martin, and I asked the following question in the paper jointly delivered in the Colloquium to which I referred in the Acknowledgements: "Does religion still condone violence against women?" The answer we received was "yes" more than "no." Monotheistic religions, in general, have not sufficiently contributed to the elimination of patriarchal structures that support violence against women, especially in the context of the family. Rosemary Radford Ruether concisely summarizes the problem in terms of women's rights and their reproductive sexuality.[59] Attempting to control women's sexuality and reproduction has been a consistent behavior within the three monotheistic religions. In the case of the Roman Catholic Church, this is a control

[59] "The denial of reproductive agency to women," she says, "is one of the perduring and most egregious forms of violence to women, causing millions of deaths, physical injuries, loss of health and destruction of human development. By denying women the moral right and the ability to choose when they will have sex and when the sexual act will impregnate them, women's lives are continually destroyed. Desperately seeking abortions under illegal and unsafe conditions, they die or are permanently injured. They are forced to submit to unwanted sex and/or unchosen pregnancies that prevent their educational development and capacity to live fuller lives.

"Children are also denied the possibility of being welcomed into families where their birth is chosen and their education and loving care is possible. All these disastrous consequences for women[,] for children, for humanity in general and its relation to world resources are denied by insisting that such passive acceptance of pregnancy and childbearing is woman's 'natural' fate and duty. Religion has been and continues to be the primary source of shaping and enforcing this ideological justification of violence to women" (Rosemary Radford Ruether, "Religion, Reproduction and Violence against Women," in Isherwood and Ruether [Eds.], *Weep Not for Your Children*, pp. 24-25; see also Elisabeth Schüssler Fiorenza, *In Memory of Her: A Feminist Theological Reconstruction of Christian Origins* [Tenth Anniversary Edition: With a New Introduction], New York: Crossroad, 1994 [©1983], pp. 350-351).

made by men and, particularly, by unmarried men! But any religious justification of violence against others, or the religious justification of needless suffering, is a most flagrant manipulative use of God's name.

There are, presently, some calls for action within religious institutions for the eradication of the violence experienced by women within the family context. In this regard the document *Violence en héritage?* speaks about the important role of the Catholic Church in educating believers against domestic violence.[60] According to this document, one of the essential tasks which would make it possible for the Church to fulfill is "[t]o integrate into the formation of future priests a sensitization to the problem of conjugal violence, its causes and its consequences, as well as a formation for an adequate pastoral intervention for this specific problem."[61] However, it is important to note that this recommendation was made in 1989. Eight years later, in 1997, as indicated by Veerle Draulans, there had not been much change in the education of priests and the prevention of violence against women:

> Another striking result can be seen from the research done among more than 300 [American and Canadian] priests [and published in 1997]: approximately one out of ten had been confronted regularly with a form of violence in families,... It is peculiar to note that only 8% of the 332 priests who were interviewed say that they have been educated to deal adequately with such situation. 37% of them said that they were not really equipped to handle, guide and take care of such situations of violence in families. A big group of those who were interviewed asked for more specific training and education, with the purpose of giving optimum support to the victims of violence in homes through counseling sessions. Nason-Clark [the director of the research] observes that this confronts us with the demand concerning the particular contribution that a pastoral counselor can make through discussions with the victims of partner violence. She advises the establishment of strong networks of interdisciplinary and professional social workers who can provide help competently and as a team.[62]

[60] See *Violence en héritage?*, pp. 45-47.

[61] *Violence en héritage?*, p. 47 (my translation).

[62] Draulans, "Human Dignity Violated by Increasing Aggression," p. 244 (referring to Nancy Nason-Clark, *The Battered Wife: How Christians Confront Family Violence*, Louisville: Westminster John Knox Press, 1997, pp. 143-148). These results are particularly shocking, taking into consideration what Draulans said shortly before on the same page: "When women who are victims of violence want to tell their story to another woman, it is mostly to another woman of the same church community whom they can trust enough that they can share their story. These women rarely make use of the secular assistance that is made available by the provincial of the municipality." Thus, if so many priests are ill-prepared to deal with domestic violence, what to think about parishioners, or believers in general?

Consequently, it is urgent for pastoral agents in the Catholic Church, as well for leaders within other religious faiths, to make the concern for domestic violence and abuse a pastoral priority. As Nienhuis says fittingly, "[t]here are a lot of issues facing religious communities, but few of them may result in the deaths of members and the destruction of their families. This one can."[63] This pastoral priority should concern not only the formation of future priests, but also and particularly, the current ones. In the Roman Catholic Church, the shortage of vocations to the priesthood, at least in the Western world, is evident, and the average age of active clergy is very high. This also means that many of them, as many other people of their age, carry with them the most patriarchal biases against women. There is, then, a strong need for a renewal of the theological presuppositions regarding women, suffering and forgiveness.[64] Within the Christian context, this formation is an urgent necessity for Church leaders, pastoral agents and believers in general, without any exception.

Within Judaism, Christianity, and Islam, we cannot conceive of a Heaven (Paradise) without at the same time thinking of a transformed creation. This implies that we are not able to live truly human lives unless we live in solidarity with nature. Living our faith to the fullest requires that we recognize that we are created in relationship with others, and in communion with the universe as a whole. This is fundamental to our heritage, here and now, to construct a more united humanity, to establish a less destructive and more respectful relationship with the entire environment in keeping with our reality as created beings and with the recognition that a "new creation" is called to endure.

In this regard, as Claude Lévi-Straus has pointed out, contrary to the biases against aboriginal peoples according to which they were considered as somehow less than human and incapable of systematic thought, aboriginal peoples have rich cultures and offer us a more "harmonious and unifying" understanding of creation and of human beings within that creation. This is contrary to the more "discordant and dualistic"

[63] Nienhuis, "Theological Reflections on Violence and Abuse," p. 109.

[64] This is what the document *Violence en héritage?* indicates, too: "[T]he Church would like to renew its theology taking into consideration the signs of the times" (p. 42 [my translation]). But it should be said better: the Church "ought to" renew it. This is so because, as Nancy Eileen Nienhuis emphasizes, "[i]f we don't challenge this understanding of God and scripture, then we are also to blame for the violence [against women]" ("Theological Reflections on Violence and Abuse," p. 20).

understanding of human nature often offered by Western thought.[65] Rather than consider human beings as the summit of everything, to which the rest of life (nature) must be submitted, Lévi-Strauss states that the inclusive conception of the world of aboriginal peoples affirms that the world (nature) exists before life and life before human beings.[66]

Ecological and feminist movements, as well, have made a major contribution to a more holistic understanding of creation. In this regard, today one of the important fields that has grown out of feminist thought is "ecofeminism." Ecofeminism's conception of the world, less possessive than that of a patriarchal worldview,[67] obliges us to see life from a different perspective, that is to say, in a more global and connected way. Western anthropology conveyed a distorted vision of human beings, considering themselves superior to others. However, Western civilization can no longer be considered the centre of the cosmos. The ecological crisis of the modern world confronts us with a disastrous relationship between the person and the environment. This crisis challenges us in our own time to build a new covenant with creation. For violence inflicted upon the environment has destructive socio-political and economical repercussions. To respect the "sacredness" of the Earth is also a particularly valuable source for living in peace.

Finally, we need to understand the "whys" hidden inside of violent actions in order to help surmount and eliminate such actions and overcome their disastrous results. Coming to such an understanding will be the purpose of the next chapter.

[65] See Claude Lévi-Strauss, *Anthropologie structurale*, Paris: Plon, 1958, pp. 113-114; Claude Lévi-Strauss, *La pensée sauvage*, Paris: Plon, 1963, pp. 50-52, 57-58.

[66] See Lévi-Strauss, *L'origine des manières de table*, p. 422.

[67] See Rosemary Radford Ruether, *Gaia and God: An Ecofeminist Theology of Earth Healing*, San Francisco: HarperSanFrancisco, 1992; Sallie McFague, *The Body of God: An Ecological Theology*, Minneapolis: Fortress Press, 1993; Haether Eaton, "Ecofeminism, Cosmology, and Spiritual Renewal," in *Église et Théology*, 29/1 (1998), pp. 115-128; Sallie McFague, "Imagining God and 'A Different World'," in *Concilium*, 5 (2004), pp. 42-50; Mary Judith Ress, *Ecofeminism in Latin America*, Maryknoll: Orbis Books (Women from the Margins), 2006, pp. 158-165, 185-191.

Chapter 4

Towards an Understanding of Religion and Violence

One day, just after my arrival in Ottawa in 1985, I was travelling in my car and turned on the radio. I began listening to a "call-in" program in which people could express their opinions on the topic of the day: "What should we do with criminal offenders?" I must confess that, because that topic deeply interested me, I paid careful attention to what people were saying. Most of them said that Canada needed harsher sentences. Some believed that offenders should be imprisoned longer and that Canada needed to build more penitentiaries. Then, a woman, who was a sociologist, intervened and said: "I am very surprised that so far no one is asking: 'Why is there an increase in criminal behavior?' 'Why is the average age of offenders decreasing?' 'What can we do, as a society, to look into the causes of violence and violent behavior in order to solve this problem or reduce its impact?'" I had the impression that the anchor of the program felt threatened since she did not know how to respond.

Since then, I have often reflected on these questions. In fact, in the United States and Canada, one major problem is the increasingly younger age of violent offenders. Social responses to this problem are often in line with the majority of those expressed on the radio program, particularly the "necessity" of treating young offenders as adults. There were indeed only a few reflections on the possible causes of the problem.

Perhaps it is time for us in the United States and in Canada to ask the same questions as those raised by the sociologist on the radio program: "As a society, are we somehow complicit in this situation?" "What are our responsibilities, as citizens, to these young offenders?" In line with our remarks in previous chapters, we can see how much easier is to demonize these young people than to reflect on the causes of the problem.

Trying to understand some of the underlying reasons for violence does not mean justifying or excusing it. On the contrary, in order to overcome violence it is essential to identify some of the motivations that trigger it, and to recognize that such a task is a social responsibility. My intention in this chapter is to present some approaches to help us better understand the motivations underlying violent behavior, particular those motivations associated with religion.

In the first approach here below I will explore the notion that the Holy Scriptures of the three monotheistic religions are divinely inspired books and how this provides some of the faithful with the perceived justification to act violently. Exploring this belief not only involves consideration of the literal and/or selective interpretation of the sacred texts, but also recognition of the fact that religious violence is not the exclusive patrimony of fundamentalists.

In the second approach I will deal with what I call "the myth of male superiority," that is, patriarchy. Here, patriarchy will be understood as the socio-cultural ideology lying behind many of the sacred texts perceived to justify violence.

The third approach will consist of an examination of these consequences of violence which are particularly related to shame, which is one of the motivations for retaliation or for responding violently to violence. Here, I consider a narcissistic personality as characteristic of people that have suffered extremely shameful situations. It is my contention that narcissism is a predominant personality trait of terrorists, people who behave violently and without any sense of guilt.

In the fourth approach I will emphasize the negative impact of globalization. I am particularly interested in an "ideological conception" of globalization that denies diversity and oppresses poor countries. These countries and their citizens are often the ones paying for the enrichment of wealthier nations.

Finally, my fifth approach will take the form of an analysis of the presence of a culture of violence, destruction and death in the West. As was discussed in the second chapter above, in such a culture, violence has become a form of "entertainment" and "distraction" used to fight against boredom.

1. The Bible and the Qur'an as Divinely Inspired Books

We easily recognize fundamentalist tendencies manifesting themselves among many believers within Judaism, Christianity, and Islam.[1] These so-called "fundamentalists" operate according to a literal and/or selective interpretation of sacred texts. As Simon John De Vries states: "I define a *Fundamentalist* as one who may claim to cling to the earliest form of a religion but who in fact has selected a feature that may not be essential,

[1] See Mooren, *War and Peace in Monotheistic Religions*, pp. 18, 137-140.

and who makes it centrally significant at the expense of what turns out to be, upon careful and unbiased investigation, the truly central and basic point of the faith."[2] This practice of selective interpretation often causes such fundamentalists to fall into intransigent and fanatical attitudes toward other believers. Sometimes fundamentalists enter into a covenant with the established powers and oppose those perceived to be their enemies, namely, those who do not share the same political and religious beliefs.[3] Thus, as Bruce B. Lawrence observes, "[f]undamentalists are oppositional. They do not merely disagree with their enemies, they confront them."[4] Fundamentalists also cannot tolerate ambiguity, individual freedom, and diversity.[5] In short, they do not respect the other and try to impose their opinions on the political and religious majority.[6]

Fundamentalists often come from affluent families or social groups, which provides them with the ability and the means to develop their own vocabulary.[7] Besides, Kurtz states, "[f]undamentalists derive their moral principles from revealed truth, as handed down in ancient times, and they are inflexible in their insistence that they are God's absolute commandments."[8] In fact, their positions can be considered religious ideologies. Furthermore, as Lawrence points out: "It is, moreover, a *religious* ideology since the beliefs of its adherents, their practices, their challenges, and aspirations, [are] all framed in discourse that authorizes action through scriptural, creedal, and moral referents."[9] These religious

[2] De Vries, "Scenes of Sex and Violence in the Old Testament," in Ellens (Ed.), *The Destructive Power of Religion*, vol. 1, p. 75.

[3] See Paul Kurtz, "The Growth of Fundamentalism Worldwide," in Academy of Humanism, *Neo-Fundamentalism: The Humanist Response*, Buffalo: Prometheus Books, 1988, p. 11.

[4] Bruce B. Lawrence, *Defender of God: The Fundamentalist Revolt against the Modern Age*, San Francisco: Harper & Row, 1989, p. 100.

[5] See Richard G. Cote, "God Sings in the Night: Ambiguity as an Invitation to Believe," in *Concilium* 4 (1992), pp. 95-105. In this article, Cote highlights the results of some research on the "psychology of intolerance": "The focus of most of this research," he says, "has been to determine how intolerance of ambiguity relates to other personality traits. The research findings have shown–indeed have shown quite convincingly–that people who are intolerant of ambiguity are more than likely to evince one or more of the following traits: low self-esteem, rigidity in thinking, close-mindedness, dogmatism, anxiety, strong ethnocentrism, religious fundamentalism, conformity, prejudice and low creativity" (pp. 97-98).

[6] See Kurtz, "The Growth of Fundamentalism Worldwide," in Academy of Humanism, *Neo-Fundamentalism*, pp. 11-12.

[7] See Lawrence, *Defenders of God*, pp. 100-101.

[8] Kurtz, "The Growth of Fundamentalism Worldwide," in Academy of Humanism, *Neo-Fundamentalism*, p. 12; see also McTernan, *Violence in God's Name*, pp. 21-22.

[9] Lawrence, *Defenders of God*, p. 97.

ideologies are dependent on socio-cultural contexts that are very clearly demarcated and influenced by complex personalities, namely, by intolerant people with a low self-esteem.

J. Harold Ellens considers fundamentalism to be a "psychopathology" that can be found in all dimensions of life, not only in religious contexts:

> An essential component of this psychology is a rigid structuralist approach that has an obsessive-compulsive flavor to it. It is the mark of those who have very limited ability to live with the ambiguity inherent to healthy human life; or have no capacity for that at all. Fundamentalism is a psychopathology that drives its proponents to the construction of orthodoxies in whatever field it is in which those proponents live or work.[10]

Moreover, Jack Nelson-Pallmeyer suggests that religious violence is not only a question of misinterpretation of texts and their misappropriation by fundamentalist extremists, but it is also related to the reality that there are toxic texts–sacred texts that carry on "pathological portraits of God," of a "warrior God" who commands violence. These texts are often taken out of context and manipulated to justify violence in the name of religion.[11]

In light of these circumstances, Nelson-Pallmeyer argues that believers themselves, within the three monotheisms, are obliged to confront the violence within their sacred texts.[12] This is also the opinion of Jacques Ellul with regard to the need for a careful interpretation of such lethal passages.[13] Confronting violence rooted in the inadequate interpretation of these passages requires dealing not only with how they are

[10] J. Harold Ellens, "Fundamentalism, Orthodoxy, and Violence," in Ellens (Ed.), *The Destructive Power of Religion*, vol. 4, p. 120; see also pp. 119, 140-141. For his part, Jamal Khader gives a very interesting description of fundamentalism: "Some common characteristics of fundamentalism," he says, "include: 1) religious idealism as the basis for personal and communal identity; 2) an understanding of truth as revealed and unified; 3) envisioning themselves as part of a cosmic struggle; 4) the seizure of historical moments and reinterpretation of them in light of a cosmic struggle; 5) the demonization of opposition; 6) selectivity in what parts of their tradition and heritage they stress" ("Opportunities and Threats for Religions in Conflict and Violence: How [Not] to Use the Name of God," in Haers, Hintersteiner and Schrijver, *Postcolonial Europe in the Crucible of Cultures*, p. 142; see also p. 159 where he underlies how fundamentalists believe to be "God's chosen" people and, as such, excluding the other who "*is not*" chosen. Thus, the chosen one is "better and superior").

[11] See Nelson-Pallmeyer, *Is Religion Killing Us?*, pp. xiv-xv, 20, 39.

[12] See Nelson-Pallmeyer, *Is Religion Killing Us?*, p. 108. In the next chapter, I deconstruct the literal interpretation of God as the true author of the Holy Scriptures.

[13] See Ellul, *Violence*, pp. 160-161.

being interpreted, but it also requires cultivating an awareness of the reality that Andrew Kille highlights:

> To understand the role of sacred scriptures in shaping violent attitudes and behavior we must recognize that texts do not do anything in themselves. It is only in the dynamic encounter between the text and a specific reader, in a specific community, in a particular historical and cultural context that individuals engage, interpret, internalize and ultimately act on those texts.[14]

It is true that, as Kille indicates, it is not texts but people who kill. However, there is also a need to acknowledge that most believers, within the three monotheistic religions, are experts neither in biblical or Qur'anic hermeneutics nor in psychology or sociology. For centuries, they have been told that their Holy Scriptures are inspired by God, that God is their true author.[15] In fact, as Nadeau and Redmond highlight in referring to the Bible, "[i]t is the text which speaks... and not the commentaries."[16] For this reason, as I will develop at greater length in

[14] D. Andrew Kille, "'The Bible Made Me Do It': Text, Interpretation, and Violence," in Ellens (Ed.), *The Destructive Power of Religion*, vol. 1, p. 56. He adds later on: "Does this lead us to the conclusion that scripture causes violence? Does a toxic text necessarily trigger paranoid reactions? Does it always support hostility and aggression? Which comes first, paranoia in the text or paranoia in the reader? Idealizations of the ingroup and outward projections of aggression onto others developed during the beginnings of a religious movement provide only potential stimuli for violence. Scriptural justifications are far more likely to be secondary phenomena, mustered to support a worldview, attitude, and ideology that are already hostile and aggressive" (p. 62). In this regard, and according to Jonathan E. Brockopp, what makes someone a terrorist is not the texts, but "intolerance." Thus, he says, "extremists like bin Laden are marked by their rejection of the pluralism embedded in the Islamic tradition. They argue that their version of history is the only one that preserves the heart of the tradition. As a result, they must be both highly selective in representing this tradition and also intolerant of contrary voices. To my mind, it is this intolerance that identifies them as extremist, purposefully living on the edge of a tradition that loves discussion and disagreement" ("Jihad and Islamic History," in Rennie and Tite [Eds.], *Religion, Terror and Violence*, pp. 145-146).

[15] Clinton Bennett makes a very important point here. For him, there is no doubt that, "since the Bible and Qur'an contain a lot of divinely sanctioned violence, it should be no surprise that Christians and Muslims act violently" (*In Search of Solutions*, p. 192). Yet, he recognizes the need to deal with these "violent scriptures" without denying that, beyond their interpretation, there is the reality of the texts: "The argument that such justification always represents a misinterpretation of scripture may be difficult to sustain, although in the writer's opinion a case can be made for this" (p. 193). This is also the position of Römer. For him, it is not only a question of proposing "allegorical" interpretations of these "violent scriptures," but to recognize the "scandalous character" of these texts (see "De meurtres et de guerres," in Marguerat [Ed.], *Dieu est-il violent?*, p. 35).

[16] Nadeau and Redmond, "Le Dieu des victimes reconsidéré à partir des victimes d'abus sexuels durant l'enfance," in Noël (Ed.), *Mondialisation, violence et religion*, p. 128 (my translation).

the next chapter, religious leaders have the moral responsibility to deal with the question of how to interpret the conception of God as the true author of the Holy Scriptures, not only from biblical and Qur'anic hermeneutical perspectives but also with catechetical and pastoral concerns in mind.

In reality, what lies behind many of these texts is the projection of a male, exclusivist vision of the world.

2. Patriarchy: The Myth of Male Superiority

In the previous chapter above, I mentioned the negative role that patriarchy plays in situations of domestic violence and with regard to the "ecological holocaust." Patriarchal attitudes can be found in many texts of the Hebrew Scriptures, which are already infused with the biased cultural sexism of their time.[17] By the third century of our era, the connection linking women and evil, based in an "ideological and patriarchal" interpretation of Genesis 3, was firmly set in the Christian ethos, as evidenced by the following text from Tertullian (ca. 155–ca. 220):

> God's sentence hangs still over all your sex and His punishment weighs down upon you. You are the devils gateway; you are she who first violated the forbidden tree and broke the law of God. It was you who coaxed your way around him whom the devil had not the force to attack. With what ease you shattered that image of God: man! Because of the death you merited the Son of God had to die. And yet you think of nothing but covering your tunics with ornaments?[18]

Even if the creation stories of Genesis (1–2) do not promote a sexist dichotomy between man and woman in themselves, at least not intentionally, the subsequent interpretations of these texts ranged from being merely ambiguous to highly prejudicial against women. These

[17] See *Violence en héritage?*, pp. 24-25; Philys Tribble, *Texts of Terror: Literary-Feminist Readings of Biblical Narratives*, Philadelphia: Fortress Press (Overtures to Biblical Theology, 13), 1984.

[18] Quintus Septimius Florens Tertullianus, *De Cultu Feminorum*, in Jacques-Paul Migne, *Patrologiae Cursus Completus: Series Latina*, Parisiis: Excudabat Migne, 1844–[196-?], vol. I, 1, cols. 304-305. As cited in Julia O'Faolain and Lauro Martines (Eds.)'s book *Not in God's Image: Women in History from the Greeks to the Victorians*, New York, Evanston, San Francisco, London (UK): Harper & Row (Harper Torchbook), 1973, p. 132.

interpretations clearly connected women with sin through Eve's "participation" in the first sin of humanity, and they affirmed that this was the meaning of the biblical texts.[19]

In the Hebrew Scriptures, one has the impression that women are often treated as chattel or property as in the case of Hagar, the slave-girl of Sara, Abraham's wife. Hagar was used, so to speak, to bear an heir for Abraham when she conceived her son Ishmael (Gen 21:8-21). Again the integrity of women as persons is disregarded with the violent rape of Tamar, Absalom's sister, by her half-brother Amnon (2 Sam 13:1-22). Consider the sexual and lethal violence against the Levite's concubine in Ephraim, who was not only systematically raped by "the men of the city" but also "cut... into twelve pieces" (Judg 19:1-30). And what can be said about Jephthah's vow to the Lord, where he offers his daughter, his only child and a virgin, as a sacrifice if he is victorious over his enemies (Judg 11:29-40)?[20] Women were considered, and counted, as the property of their husbands (Ex 20:17; Deut 5:21; 24:1-2) and were subjected to the authority of their fathers, brothers, husbands and brothers-in-law (Deut 25:5-10). They also had no legal rights, and their activities and participation in worship in the Temple and the Synagogue were restricted. Within this context, it is easy to imagine the purpose behind and the reason why male Jews daily thanked God with the words: "I thank you for having made me neither a pagan, nor woman, nor ignorant."[21]

[19] Chapter 3 of Genesis tells us about the disobedience of the first human couple, Adam and Eve (this is the "sin at the origins"). This is a "sin" that presents to us, in a symbolic language, the breaking of creation's harmony. It was not a question of affirming that every human being comes into the world with a personal, constitutive stain, but of describing, symbolically, a sinful situation that precedes the human being and characterizes all human relationships and creation. Unfortunately, Christian tradition, after Saint Augustine, speaks of an inherited "original sin" that affects us ontologically, that is, as constitutive of human beings. The difference between the "sin at the origins" and the "original sin" is therefore essential: we have moved from a symbolic situation to an ontological reality. This is why the two can no longer continue to be identified, even though it is recognized that both of them refer to the event of a first sin by humanity according to Genesis 3. A situation that has been expressed symbolically cannot be translated ontologically without making relevant changes. In interpreting the "sin at the origins" in an ontological manner, "original sin," Christian tradition has gone farther than what is described in Genesis 3 (see Martínez de Pisón, *Sin and Evil*, pp. 69-96).

[20] See Nelson-Pallmeyer, *Is Religion Killing Us?*, p. 35.

[21] This prayer is cited in *Violence en héritage?*, p. 25 (my translation); see also Schüssler Fiorenza, *In Memory of Her*, p. 217, where she develops the "cultural pattern" underlying this form of prayer "not only among Jews but among Greeks and Romans as well."

As Tatha Wiley points out, these interpretations are the result of "patriarchal gender ideologies" that forget Jesus' proclamation of the equality among human beings.[22] It was Jesus who challenged patriarchy and introduced a revolution regarding the socio-cultural order of his time concerning women.[23] Jesus' public life is full of women-disciples who followed him. He speaks freely with them, as was the case with the woman of Samaria (Jn 4:1-42). Jesus treats them with dignity and respect, as on the occasion of the woman caught in adultery (Jn 7:53–8:11). Risen from the dead, Jesus appears initially to a group of women (Mk 16:1-8; see also Mt 18:1-8; Lk 24:1-11; Jn 20:1-18). Even Saint Paul in his Letter to the Galatians makes explicit the socio-cultural and religious revolution brought about by Jesus when he affirms: "There is no longer Jew or Greek, there is no longer slave or free, there is no longer male and female; for all of you are one in Christ Jesus" (Gal 3:28).[24] Yet, Jesus' revolution regarding women and their status dissipated too soon. The growing tension concerning the control of women and their charisma is evident in the early Church, as witnessed to in Paul's First Letter to Timothy (1 Tim 3:16). The suppression of the "Order of Widows" and the discontinuing of the practice of ordaining deaconesses in the fourth century show the extent to which the radical practices of Jesus and the early Church communities had succumbed to the pressures of patriarchy.[25] Patriarchal culture was very powerful, as can be seen in the Letter of Saint Paul to the Ephesians, where in the Letter women are instructed to be submissive to their husbands: "Wives, be subject to your husbands as you are to the Lord. For the husband is the head of the wife just as Christ is the head of the church, the body of which he is the Savior. Just as the church

[22] See Tatha Wiley, *Original Sin: Origins, Developments, Contemporary Meanings*, New York: Paulist Press, 2002, pp. 153-178.

[23] See Marie Jo Thiel, "Femmes dans l'Église du Christ," in *La Documentation catholique*, 2368 (2006), pp. 1021-1023; *Violence en héritage?*, pp. 25-26; Schüssler Fiorenza, *In Memory of Her*, pp. 140-151; see also pp. 160-204 where Schüssler Fiorenza presents the recognition of women and their equality with men in the early Christian missionary movement.

[24] See Schüssler Fiorenza, *In Memory of Her*, pp. 205-241.

[25] See John Wijngaards, "The History of Women Deacons/Deaconesses," at http://www.womenpriests.org/deacons/deac_his.asp (accessed September 28, 2011); Hamilton Hess, "Changing Forms of Ministry in the Early Church," in James A. Coriden (Ed.), *Sexim and Church Law: Equal Rights and Affirmative Action*, New York: Paulist Press, 1977, pp. 43-57; Schüssler Fiorenza, *In Memory of Her*, pp. 243-342; M. Cathleen Kaveny, "The Order of Widows: What the Early Church Can Teach Us about Older Women and Health," in *Christian Bioethics*, 11 (2005), pp. 11-34.

is subject to Christ, so also wives ought to be, in everything, to their husbands" (Eph 5:22-24).[26]

The same evolution toward more negative attitudes toward women can be found in Islam. It is true that, as Hans Küng says, "[i]n principle in the Qur'an husband and wife are equal before God, because both have been created by God."[27] Küng refers to two Suras. The first one says: "It is He Who created you from a single person, and made his mate of like nature, in order that he might dwell with her (in love). When they are united, she bears a light burden and carries it about (unnoticed). When she grows heavy, they both pray to Allah their Lord, (saying): 'If Thou givest us a goodly child, we vow we shall (ever) be grateful'" (7:189).

The second Sura continues in the same vein: "(He is) the Creator of the heavens and the earth: He has made for you pairs from among yourselves, and pairs among cattle: by this means does He multiply you: there is nothing whatever like unto Him, and He is the One that hears and sees (all things)" (42:11; see also S 16:97; 33:35). Yet, later on, in spite of the recognition of the equality of men and women in some texts of the Qur'an, within Islamic tradition and culture patriarchy dominated as well and the situation of women in Islam became not so different from those in Judaism and Christianity.[28]

In summary, despite the equality between man and woman suggested in the creation narratives of Genesis (1–2), the liberating and revolutionary attitude of Jesus on women, the equality between men and women proclaimed by Saint Paul in Galatians, as well as the equality announced in the Qur'an, there remains in the three monotheistic traditions a pervasive undercurrent of prejudice and bias against women that has not changed quickly or easily. The myth of male superiority has not fully disappeared. For this reason, as Jacques Haers says, "[t]oday gender issues have become global and very complex challenges, as we have come to discover how worldwide injustices and exploitation are 'gendered' and how closely linked they are to the construction of sociocultural identities and human self-understanding."[29] For example, the

[26] See Nienhuis, "Theological Reflections on Violence and Abuse," pp. 114-120; Nason-Clark, "When Terror Strikes at Home," p. 304.

[27] Küng, *Islam*, p. 157.

[28] In the Qur'an, as it is in the Hebrew Scriptures and in the New Testament, there are also texts that carry on patriarchal-biased conceptions of women (see, for example, S 2:223, 228, 236, 282; 4:15, 34, 128; 12:28; 24:31; 33:50, 59; 43:18; 65:1; 111:4-5).

[29] Haers, "Introduction," in Haers, Hintersteiner and Schrijver (Eds.), *Postcolonial Europe in the Crucible of Cultures*, p. 8.

almost exclusively male categories that have been projected onto God, as a result of a patriarchal culture, have negatively influenced women's spiritual development. In particular, this has had an impact on women's ability to find their own ways of relating to God.

From a psychological perspective, Leona Stucky-Abbott shows how the use of almost exclusively male images of God has influenced the development of the identity of women.[30] When believers create a male image of God and then project it onto God, stressing dimensions of the human that are typically male, such as power, force, strength, and the like, women will not recognize this image and these characteristics in themselves. They will recognize their identity as women by learning that, unlike men, they do not have these male characteristics. In short, the identity of women is negatively affected by the image and characteristics of this male God. Therefore, they will feel diminished in their identity.[31] Thus, from the starting point of a patriarchal culture, a male God has been created who hinders women from developing their own ways of experiencing the Divine on the basis of what they more positively recognize in themselves.

One of the results of patriarchy is the violence that women have endured "since the beginning of the world." As Francisco Díez de Velasco indicates, this violence is the result of

> the privilege of gender, a structural violence that justifies the subordinate position of women.... Examples of this can be found in the exercise of religious leadership in the Catholic, Orthodox, Judaic and Islamic faiths and in that of full monastic consecration, as in Theravada Buddhism. Such a violence can even result in death, as in the Indian *sati* ritual, the funeral sacrifice in which the wife must accompany her husband, joining him on his death journey (but never the other way around).[32]

Patriarchy traverses cultures, chronological successions, and religions. To come to terms with this fact we need to recognize the patriarchal biases that are present in religious understandings and texts and that impact on the ways women and the LGBTQ community are treated.[33]

[30] See Leona Stucky-Abbott, "The Impact of Male God Imagery on Female Identity Meaning," in *The Journal of Pastoral Care*, 47 (1993), p. 241.

[31] See Stucky-Abbott, "The Impact of Male God Imagery on Female Identity Meaning," pp. 243-244.

[32] Díez de Velasco, "Theoretical Reflection on Violence and Religion," p. 102; see also p. 103.

[33] See Juergensmeyer, *Terror in the Mind of God*, pp. 200-201.

In conclusion, gendered violence and patriarchal-biased conceptions of women and those of different sexual orientations are still very much alive today. Lisa Isherwood discusses the state of such patriarchal conceptions within the Christian tradition. It is worth quoting her entire passage to underscore the urgency of deconstructing patriarchy:

> As a sobering legacy for those who claim Christian marriage to be the pinnacle of human relationship we have Christian marriage manuals of the 1960s which read more like rapist manuals than lessons in loving mutuality. They encourage the muscular Christian to take his wife by force the first time so as to set the tone of the marriage and put in place the power relations. He is told she will object and may feel pain but will be glad of it in the end, as she can feel safe in the knowledge that he is in charge. Sex [is] then used as a weapon to create and maintain the gendered roles within the marriage and far beyond into the public arena. The connection of this to the wider political scene can be shown through the objections of some Members of Parliament to the efforts of Marie Stoppes to provide safe contraception for women. One outraged Member of Parliament said such things would breed a generation of effeminate men who would not be able to discharge their duties in the Empire–a clear and rather Freudian link there I think! We see similar patterns promoted by the True Love Waits campaign, it is true they do not advocate the implied violence of the 1960s marriage manuals but they do make it clear that sex is something that the husband decides on and interviews with the young men show how they anticipate sex 24/7 once they are married. Where are the women and their desire in this I wonder?[34]

This "patriarchal gender ideology," to use Wiley's expression, has not only affected the relationships between human beings but also their relationship with creation. The Hebrew Scriptures speak about the goodness and beauty of everything that is created. As a result of patriarchal culture and its influence, however, a dualistic and Manichean conception of creation has emerged in monotheistic religions. If creation is the "very good" work of Yahweh (Gen 1:31), what then explains the far too common negative conception of creation that perpetuates destructive human behavior toward it?

Greek philosophy espouses a dualistic, Manichean, cosmology and anthropology that was, generally speaking, completely alien to the Hebrew Scriptures. For the Greek philosopher, Plato (ca. 427–ca. 347 B.C.), as for Aristotle (384–322 B.C.) after him, the world and concrete

[34] Isherwood, "The Violence of Gender," in Isherwood and Ruether (Eds.), *Weep Not for Your Children*, pp. 58-59.

human experience do not have value in themselves. Rather, human beings exist in and as a dualistically conceived reality: spirit and matter. Out of this epistemology, there developed a dichotomous idea of human beings as composed of body and soul. The body, as creation in general, was considered evil. Material things acquired their value only through their reference to a superior entity: God and, by deduction, the spirit (soul).[35]

This dualistic and Manichean vision appears for the first time in the Hebrew Scriptures with the book of the Wisdom of Solomon (1st century B.C.). This book employs a dualistic conception of the human being: a soul separated from the body as the recipient of immortality. Tradition interprets this book as written under the influence of the Hellenistic culture of that time. With it, a different anthropological language appeared in the Hebrew Scriptures.

Another step in the development of the Hellenistic conception of the world's overall negative influence consists in the Cartesian male-oriented primacy of reason that characterizes Western thought from early to late Modernity (15th–20th centuries). René Descartes' (1596–1650) statement, "Cogito, ergo sum" ("I think, therefore I am") has been made famous.[36] For Descartes, the body belongs to what he calls in Latin the "rex extensa," that is to say, the things that are extended, as external to reason, as a kind of instrument to be used, controlled and dominated by the soul, by the spirit.[37] The "rex extensa," namely, material, created, things, do not have value in themselves but only as related to the spirit.[38] The primacy of reason continued well into the twentieth century.

The consequences of this dualism for the conception of nature, creation, anthropology and corporeality are indeed fundamentally negative. Dualism allowed for the patriarchal primacy of reason (spirit) over matter. Ironically, reason became a kind of "goddess" to whom everything

[35] See John Watson, *The Interpretation of Religious Experience* (The Gifford Lectures, 1910–1912), vol. 1 (Historical), New York: AMS Press, 1979 (©1912), pp. 9, 12, 17, 20; Ramón Martínez de Pisón, *God: From Knowing to Experiencing*, Toronto: Novalis Publishing Inc., 2009, pp. 25-39; Rapley, *The Lord as Their Portion*, p. 60.

[36] See Richard A. Watson, *Cogito, Ergo Sum: The Life of René Descartes*, Boston: David R. Godine, 2007 (©2002).

[37] See René Descartes, "Méditation sixième: De l'existence des choses matérielles, et de la réelle distinction entre l'âme et le corps de l'homme," in René Descartes, *Œuvres philosophiques: Tome II (1638–1642)*, Paris: Garnier Frères (Classiques Garnier), 1967, pp. 487-488; see also Benoît Garceau, "Ethnologie structuraliste et connaissance de l'homme," in *Science et Esprit*, XXXIV/1 (1982), pp. 9-10; Anne Fortin, "Violence et retour au même: Les résistances du trinitaire," in Noël (Ed.), *Mondialisation, violence et religion*, pp. 137-139.

[38] See Primavesi, *Gaia's Gift*, pp. 78-82.

else was subdued. As a result, the Bible's unitary and positive ideas of creation and of the conception of human beings disappeared. Goodness and beauty belonged to reason. Only by extension, by participation in the exercise of reason, could human beings find some reflection of goodness and beauty in nature. Everything external to the spirit (soul) was considered as an instrument to be used, and as fundamentally bad.

"Patriarchal gender ideologies," which negatively affect women, the LGBTQ community, and creation, are still very present today.[39] Consequently, there is a need to overcome such ideologies for promoting gender equality, a point to which I will return in the next chapter.

3. Shame and the Spiral of Violence

In the previous chapter, I explored the notion of humiliation as a consequence of violence, while recognizing that many different factors may trigger humiliation. Humiliation is, however, a particularly important consequence of violence because it is one of the sources of shame which, in turn, can lead to further violence. But what is shame?[40]

Shame is among the least studied of the emotions which affect human development. In order to better understand shame, the first thing that we must consider is the difference between shame and guilt. Shame is not guilt. Shame reaches to the core of the person in a way that actions and a resultant sense of guilt do not. Guilt does not affect the person as a whole, but is limited to one's actions, as it is generated by "the fear of punishment and abandonment for the violation of moral values."[41] Hellen B. Lewis describes the role of the self in shame and guilt in the following terms:

> *Shame is about the self; guilt is about things*. Shame thus appears to be a "narcissistic" reaction evoked by a lapse from the ego ideal. An ego ideal is difficult to spell out rationally; shame thus can be a subjective, "irrational" reaction. Shame is about the whole self and is therefore "global". Guilt is more specific, being about events or things.

[39] Marie Andrée Roy makes it very clear. For her, the present exclusion of women from important positions within the hierarchical structures of religions is a clear "form of violence. [For this reason, some people] suggest to women that they should leave their religions because they are intrinsically patriarchal and irreformable" ("La sacralisation du pouvoir mâle," in *Relations*, 744 [2010], p. 15 [my translation]; see also p. 16).

[40] See Martínez de Pisón, *Death by Despair*, pp. 7-22; Ramón Martínez de Pisón, "Shame, Death, and Dying," in *Pastoral Psychology*, 51/1 (2002), pp. 28-31.

[41] Carl Goldberg, *Understanding Shame*, Northvale, London (UK): Jason Aronson Inc., 1991, p. 55.

> Adults regard shame as an "irrational" reaction that is more appropriate to childhood, especially if it occurs outside the context of moral transgression.[42]

Shame is conditioned by genetic-biological predispositions and by socio-historical, cultural, religious, gender, and age contexts. While shame is usually looked at negatively, there is also a positive and healthy side to shame. In this sense, shame plays an essential role in human development. It constitutes a protection of the self and of one's personal identity in adverse circumstances, and it sets boundaries or limits that human beings should not trespass. In this sense, too, one can consider more specifically the role that shame plays in religion. As Helen B. Lewis says, "[i]n our Judeo-Christian heritage, shame, in the sense of humility, was (is) a principal emotion governing a person's loving relationship to God, as the story of Job attests. Job refused to blame God or himself for God's 'rejection' of him, preferring to remain humble and still loving."[43] This coincides with John Bradshaw's position regarding healthy shame. "Healthy shame," he says, "is the psychological foundation of humility. It is the source of spirituality."[44] Therefore, this first dimension or even form of shame is called modesty, humility, and respect or discretion shame, that is, "[i]t acts as an internalised defender of treasured social attitudes, values and behaviours."[45] Moreover, the consciousness of one's own fragility and vulnerability as a human being, together with the process of learning and maturing, are factors that generate a healthy sense of shame.

More commonly, shame is considered as having a degrading, dysfunctional, and pathological influence in a person's life. The adverse consequences of what can here be called chronic, toxic or unhealthy shame appear in some of the well-known attitudes of the shame-prone person: "The desire to hide or to disappear.... Embarrassment and shyness.... The feeling that one is no good, inadequate, unworthy. It is a global statement by the self in relation to the self. And... we become the object

[42] Hellen B. Lewis, "Introduction: Shame–The 'Sleeper' in Psychopathology," in Hellen B. Lewis (Ed.), *The Role of Shame in Symptom Formation*, Hillsdale, London (UK): Laurence Erlbaum Associates, 1987, p. 18.

[43] Lewis, "Introduction," in Lewis (Ed.), *The Role of Shame in Symptom Formation*, p. 3.

[44] John Bradshaw, *Healing the Shame that Binds You*, Deerfield Beach: Health Communications, Inc., 1988, p. vii.

[45] Stephen Pattison, *Shame: Theory, Therapy, Theology*, Cambridge (UK): Cambridge University Press, 2000, p. 84.

as well as the subject of shame."[46] Although more generally arising in infancy and childhood, "shame may and does occur in every stage of human development. Moreover, there appears to be no distinct, common source for the acquisition of shame."[47] Thus, according to Pattison,

> [a]ny experiences that induce a sense of persistent inferiority, worthlessness, abandonment, weakness, abjection, unwantedness, violation, defilement, stigmatisation, unlovability and social exclusion are likely to be generative of chronic shame. Perhaps the lowest common denominator in all the factors outlined here is the experience of human individuals being dishonoured, disrespected or objectified. It is this kind of experience, from infancy onwards, that engenders people whose personalities, characters and attitudes are fundamentally shaped by chronic shame.[48]

Consequently, it is important not to speak about shame as having only one source or cause; rather, there are a variety of sources that favor its emergence and give rise to it in a person. As Pattison indicates, one needs "to address the social and political factors that create and exploit an unhelpful sense of shame and alienation on the level of institutions and communities."[49] This involves unmasking the negative consequences that shame plays in serving to reinforce social, cultural and/or religious control. However, independently of its origins and socio-cultural and religious conditionings, chronic shame plays a very negative role in human and spiritual development, keeping the person feeling diminished in relationships to the self, others, and God. When a person experiences chronic, toxic shame, that person feels inadequate and in a sense defective as a whole, exposed to invasive and negative evaluation by others.

Shame is often not explicitly recognized by its name but by its influence in people's behaviors. This is what is called "bypassed" shame. According to Michael Lewis, two emotions result from unowned, bypassed, shame: "sadness" and "anger."[50] Both produce symptoms that are similar to those of what we more overtly recognize as shame, namely, feeling bad, self-blame, pain, and so forth. Furthermore, sadness, anger and even rage, "which is uncontrolled anger,"[51] emerge in a social con-

[46] Michael Lewis, *Shame: The Exposed Self*, New York: The Free Press, 1992, p. 34.
[47] Goldberg, *Understanding Shame*, p. 25.
[48] Pattison, *Shame*, p. 108.
[49] Pattison, *Shame*, p. 155.
[50] See Lewis, *Shame*, p. 120.
[51] Pattison, *Shame*, 127.

text, particularly in relationships with significant others, from a sense of "unowned" or "bypassed" shame.

For such reasons as these, Melvin R. Lansky accentuates the danger of bypassed shame in the therapeutic process, especially the need to be attentive to the fact and existence of this type of shame.[52] The inability or the unwillingness to recognize chronic, toxic shame leads people to react to their feelings in inappropriate ways. They often consider their life a failure, avoid reference to important events, deny the facts that affect them, cover-up things or behave in a secretive way, are embarrassed or humiliated, feel very vulnerable or powerless or exposed to others and their critique. In summary, these situations can further degenerate into ones in which we experience isolation, evasion, sadness, depression, self-contempt, self-attack or self-hatred, low self-esteem, inferiority, envy, anger, rage, aggression, arrogance, sarcasm, criticism, blaming others, cynicism, violence, abusiveness and manipulation in relationships, as well as into perfectionism, grandiosity, dissociative identity disorders (previously called multiple personality disorders), and pathological narcissistic personalities.

In the previous chapter above, I noted Thomas F. Homer-Dixon referring to the fact that, at the same time that "environmental scarcity" results from the exploitation of the environment, those involved in such exploitation risk entering into a process social scientists call "reciprocal causation." This term refers to the fact that in this process scarcity becomes a source of additional economic and socio-political violence.[53] "Reciprocal causation" happens with shame as well. If shame is one of the results of violence, once it is present, it risks becoming an additional source of violence. In this way, shame helps perpetuate violent behavior.

There are two ways to recognize this spiral of shame and violence. First, the violence that shame engenders is directed toward the self, with the most extreme consequences being suicide, or attempts at suicide. This is Michael Lewis' theory: "Suicide is likely to be the result of shame associated with rage directed inward.... As murder is the outward manifestation of the shame-rage spiral, suicide is its inward manifestation."[54] For instance, the relationship between bypassed

[52] See Melvin R. Lansky, "Shame and the Problem of Suicide: A Family Systems Perspective," *British Journal of Psychotherapy*, 7/3 (1991), pp. 230-242.

[53] See Homer-Dixon, *Environmental Scarcity and Violence*, pp. 6-7.

[54] Lewis, *Shame*, p. 161.

shame and suicide in children and adolescents is well documented.[55] According to Marttunen, Aro and Lönnquvist, humiliating events, such as physical and sexual abuse, in themselves already sources of shame may actually bring about suicide or attempts at suicide among children and adolescents.[56] In a particular way, Alec Roy emphasizes how childhood traumas, such as "emotional abuse, physical abuse, sexual abuse, emotional neglect, and physical neglect,"[57] are important determining factors leading later on to suicide among alcoholic populations. According to him, "[t]his is noteworthy as recent studies report significant relationships between childhood trauma and both major depression and personality disorder as an adult, two common comorbidities in alcoholics which are also associated with suicidal behavior."[58]

In conclusion to these remarks, we can note that the relationship between violence, psychological, physical, or sexual abuse of children and adolescents, and suicide is well documented. More specifically, in contemporary societies, physical and sexual abuse of children and adolescents has become a matter of real concern. If we take into account that abuse perpetrated against these groups of young people frequently has lethal consequences, becoming possible factors in suicide or generating violent behavior later on, it is not difficult for us to see that society has a responsibility in preventing violence, particularly against children and adolescents.

Second, in addition to violence enacted against oneself, the spiral of violence that shame triggers finds further expression when violence is directed toward others,[59] terrorism being one of the most extreme

[55] See Mauri J. Marttunen, Hillevi M. Aro and Jouko K. Lönnqvist, "Precipitan Stressors in Adolescent Suicide," *Journal of the American Academy of Child and Adolescent Psychiatry*, 32/6 (1993), pp. 1178-1183. In the previous chapter above, I mentioned that homophobic attitudes against the LGBTQ community can trigger suicide, and/or suicidal attempts among this group (see Beautrais, "Risk Factors for Suicide and Attempted Suicide among Young People," p. 424).

[56] In fact, sexual abuse is always a cause of humiliation and shame which generates, according to Jack T. Hanford, "an intense spiritual and social need. Shame might be deep within the psyche, the soul" ("Destructive and Constructive Religion in Relation to Shame and Terror," in Ellens [Ed.], *The Destructive Power of Religion*, vol. 2, p. 248).

[57] Alec Roy, "Brief Reports," in *The Journal of Nervous and Mental Disease*, 189/2 (2001), p. 120.

[58] Roy, "Brief Reports," p. 121.

[59] Primo Levi, the holocaust survivor already mentioned in the previous chapter above, speaks about the destruction of human dignity, that is, the humiliation and shame that prisoners, in the concentration camps during the Nazis occupation in several countries of Europe, experienced. However, what was still more painful was the fact

manifestations of this form of violence. Being humiliated and ashamed is one of the reasons that has been suggested as to why terrorists react violently, out of frustration and rage. They view violence as a way of retaliating against those who they consider responsible for their humiliating and shaming experiences. As Juergensmeyer states,

> [i]n the cases that we have examined, however, it appears that the combination of factors has made a difference, as has the intensity with which these factors are experienced and the availability of a religious and political vocabulary with which the frustrations can be articulated. Most important is the intimacy with which the humiliation is experienced and the degree to which it is regarded as a threat to one's personal honor and respectability. These can create the conditions for a desperate need for empowerment, which, when no other options appear to be open, are symbolically and violently expressed.[60]

When humiliation is very extreme, when one's dignity is not recognized, these painful experiences become potential sources of violence.[61] Thus, as Redekop says: "We have explored, initially, the role of emotions in relation to human identity needs. It has become clear that attacking, threatening, or removing need satisfiers for meaning, connectedness, action, security, and recognition can result in anger, grief, depression, fear, and shame, respectively."[62] Furthermore, when considering the relationship between shame and terrorism, it is important to take into account Jack T. Hanford's thesis: "Men [males] are socialized to deny shame and humiliation, and these powerful emotions erupt in rage, and often in a cycle of these feelings projected in violence."[63]

The spiral of violence, humiliation→toxic shame→violent retaliation, is a very common motivator in terrorist actions. Speaking about the "social-psychological dynamics of religions" supporting the terrorist

that, oftentimes, some of the prisoners who collaborated with the Nazis could behave in a more terrible way than the Nazis themselves did. This is, perhaps, one of the most patent ways of recognizing how, once human dignity is broken, victims can enter into the same spiral of violence to which I am referring here (see "The Gray Zone," in Scherper-Hughes and Bourgois [Eds.], *Violence in War and Peace*, pp. 84-85).

[60] Juergensmeyer, *Terror in the Mind of God*, p. 195; see also pp. 187-188, 191.

[61] See Ellul, *Violence*, pp. 92, 104; Redekop, *From Violence to Blessing*, pp. 23, 46, 61.

[62] Redekop, *From Violence to Blessing*, p. 155; see also pp. 164-165.

[63] Jack T. Hanford, "Destructive and Constructive Religion in Relation to Shame and Terror," in Ellens (Ed.), *The Destructive Power of Religion*, vol. 2, p. 236; see also p. 237.

attacks on September 11, 2001, Hanford says: "In the search for an answer, we will explore the power, yet neglect, of frustrating and unhealthy shame that motivates anger-rage, producing violence, wrapped up in interpretations of Christianity, Judaism, and Islamic religion, especially their radical and Fundamentalist renditions."[64] LeRoy H. Aden is another author who clearly links violence to strong negative emotions such as shame. For example, when a person feels slighted, that person often perceives violence as the most logical response to an alleged insult.[65] In short, as Juergensmeyer stresses, "terrorism has been a response to humiliation–a point that I have made throughout this book."[66] It is for these reasons that, in the next chapter, I will return to, and deal with, the need to heal the negative influences of chronic, toxic shame in order to overcome the spiral of violence.

Finally, it is important to recognize the link between shame and narcissism.[67] Melvin R. Lansky points out that, "[t]he ego ideal, that is, the standard in the face of which one might fail or be rejected, is the locus of shame."[68] He adds,

> [n]arcissistic pathology implies pathology of the ego ideal, of aspirations that are excessively harsh or unattainable rather than prohibitions.... Narcissistic pathology, by tolerating no discrepancy between the real and the ideal self, includes (and perhaps derives from) a pathological intolerance of shame. Accompanying this ego ideal pathology is the pathological need for a feeling of self-sufficiency, paradoxically accompanied by a need for others to affirm one's idealized views of

[64] Hanford, "Destructive and Constructive Religion in Relation to Shame and Terror," in Ellens (Ed.), *The Destructive Power of Religion*, vol. 2, p. 239. He adds later on: "This first section suggests that shame-anger-rage produce violence and terror. Shame unrecognized [bypassed shame] tends to blame others including their view of religion and education. The religion of the Taliban was perfectionist to the extreme, 'puritanical' superego sense, which correlates with perfectionist shame. Thus dysfunctional shame reinforced destructive religion, which reinforced judgmental shame. Education by the Taliban was used to impose their interpretation of their religion and they took over the state. Destructive shame, religion in the form of Fundamentalism, fanaticism, and anti-intellectualism became a vicious cycle in Afghanistan and perhaps in America" (pp. 240-241). All the characteristics pointed out by Hanford in referring to the "religion of the Taliban" are already indicators of the "narcissistic personality" which, according to me, as I will mention later on below, is typical of many terrorists, including Osama bin Laden.

[65] See LeRoy H. Aden, "The Role of Self-Justification in Violence," in Ellens (Ed.), *the Destructive Power of Religion*, vol. 2, p. 256.

[66] Juergensmeyer, *Terror in the Mind of God*, p. 209.

[67] See Martínez de Pisón, *Death by Despair*, pp. 36-39.

[68] Melvin R. Lansky, "Shame and Suicide in Sophocles' *Ajax*," in *Psychoanalytic Quarterly*, LXV/4 (1996), p. 769.

> oneself. Dependent on others for affirmation and accolades, such people are unable to tolerate the shame of acknowledging their true feelings of dependency on others and thus make pathological attempts to rid themselves of those feelings.[69]

As Lansky indicates, we find an "idealization" of one's self as a way of bypassing shame and, as a consequence, of arriving at the possibility of acting violently, an unhealthy way of feeling liberated from these negative emotions. For the same reasons, narcissistic people can become arrogant and frequently have the tendency to put others down, to make them feel ashamed and insignificant in order to assure that they themselves can feel superior. In so doing, they falsely idealize their own sense of themselves and who they are. According to Lansky, "very little has been published in the psychoanalytic literature on the sequences of narcissistic injury giving rise to shame and rageful attempts to restore a balance, often by attacking parties not at all involved in the original shaming and often at the cost of continued or enhanced rejection and more shame."[70] Narcissism, then, is like substance abuse in that it is a maladaptive way of dealing with chronic shame. When withdrawal is

[69] Lansky, "Shame and Suicide in Sophocles' *Ajax*," p. 769.

[70] Lansky, "Shame and Suicide in Sophocles' *Ajax*," pp. 770-771. This is also corroborated by Donald L. Nathanson. According to him, narcissism is a way of withdrawing from the painful experience of shame, that is, "narcissism is the system through which personal attributes are exaggerated in order to avoid shame" (*Shame and Pride: Affect, Sex, and the Birth of the Self*, New York, London [UK]: W. W. Norton & Company, Inc., 1992, p. 348). He does not completely accept the Freudian theory regarding the fact that narcissism is a normal step in infant development. For Nathanson, infants are not completely concerned with self-regard; rather, they communicate with their mother "through the language of innate affect" (p. 348). He continues: "If we recognize that the normal infant is never narcissistic, it becomes clear that adult narcissism is only and always a protection against shame. Narcissism is the name we give to the broad array of scripts through which people prevent themselves from 'knowing' about anything that might increase an already unbearable amount of shame" (p. 348). Pathological narcissism, with its link to shame and violence, has also been discussed by Stewert L. Hockenberry: "[T]the narcissistic personality has been described as suffering from a poorly developed self-concept and chronically low self-esteem, in which a complex range of compensatory defenses are mobilized in order to avoid further experiences of self-fragmentation, shame, and depression.... Included among these defenses are a grandiose sense of self-importance, pseudoautonomy (defensive self-sufficiency), a compulsive need to be prized and admired by others, and a need to control others as objects or extensions of oneself. These individuals characteristically approach relationships with a sense of entitlement, a lack of empathy, and a tendency to react with rage when shamed or criticized. In fact, shame and rage have both been identified as principal affects experienced within narcissistic pathology" ("Dyadic violence, Shame, and Narcisssism," in *Contemporary Psychoanalysis*, 31/2 [1995] pp. 302-303). Thus, narcissism, as a consequence of chronic shame, may bring people to behave violently.

not possible, when one feels that one's perceived deficient self is disclosed, self-inflicted violence, such as suicide, or violence directed towards others, such as terrorism, may become the final act of the wounded self. Both of these two reactions are distorted ways of struggling for self-empowerment. Thus, as Hanford says, "[w]hile destructive religion empowers violence and the punch of terrorism, the power of terror and violence in turn reciprocates by giving recognition, prestige, and importance to small groups of dissident terrorists."[71] In this regard, Charles K. Bellinger, commenting on Gilligan's position on violence,[72] says that, "[t]he violent person who is overwhelmed by shame is attempting to establish 'justice' from his [her] point of view, one that is warped by the narcissistic malformation of his [her] soul."[73]

In summary, narcissistic personalities "idolize" themselves, giving rise to an "imaginary and divinized" ego onto which they project various characteristics in order to compensate for their own lack of self-esteem. As Richard G. Cote has indicated, they manifest an intolerance of ambiguity, close-mindedness, dogmatism, and ethnocentrism.[74] These personality traits are common in the psychological profile of many of the best known terrorists.

4. "Ideological Conception" of Globalization

Jacques Racine has written a theological reflection on "the forms of violence that emerge from globalization." In this regard, and taking into consideration its negative connotations, Racine understands globalization to be an "ideology"

> that allows a dominant class to reap for itself the advantages of globalization... in order to foster outcomes that are favourable to them. This ideology serves a politico-economical totalitarianism that obeys

[71] Hanford, "Destructive and Constructive Religion in Relation to Shame and Terror," in Ellens (Ed.), *The Destructive Power of Religion*, vol. 2, p. 237.

[72] See James Gilligan, *Violence: Reflections on a National Epidemic*, New York: Vintage Books, 1996, pp. 65-66.

[73] Charles K. Bellinger, *The Genealogy of Violence: Reflections on Creation, Freedom, and Evil*, Oxford (UK): Oxford University Press, 2001, p. 92; see also Martin Kavka, "The Meaning of That Hour: Prophecy, Phenomenology, and the Public Sphere in the Early Writings of Abraham Joshua Heschel," in Clayton Crockett (Ed.), *Religion and Violence in a Secular World: Toward a New Political Theology*, Charlottesville, London (UK): University of Virginia Press (Studies in Religion and Culture), 2006, pp. 108-109.

[74] See Cote, "God Sings in the Night," pp. 97-98.

> to the logic of the market: a logic of unlimited profit, that reinforces the strong and debilitates the weak, eventuating its exclusion from the system.[75]

This ideological conception of globalization denies diversity and oppresses the poor. In particular, Racine develops four forms of violence rooted in globalization.[76] In what follows, I summarize Racine's position to bring out the negative consequences of globalization so ideologically seen.

The first form of violence Racine develops is that of violence seen and understood as a result of the "merchandizing, excluding and biogenetic engineering of the human being." Here, human beings are not considered as humans, that is, with their dignity intact, but as objects that can be bought and sold according to the whims of the market. This attitude can be seen in the transfer of technology to poor countries, where salaries are lower than in the developed world. Children are exploited in low paying jobs and women are used as sexual objects.[77] In fact, the developed world assists in the triumph of capital over human beings when cheap consumer goods are valued more than human dignity. In these circumstances, "the views of God regarding man [and woman], as expressed by Jesus Christ, are eradicated; it is God's project that is put aside by an ideology that is founded on competition without any limit."[78]

The second form of violence arising out of ideological globalization is the "homogenization of the world." The "catholicity," namely recognition of the diversity of the world's peoples, is diluted, if not suppressed. This homogenization can be considered a kind of new colonization that establishes a standardized world which fosters the consumption of

[75] Jacques Racine, "Les formes de violence émergeant de la mondialisation," in Noël (Ed.), *Mondialisation, violence et religion*, p. 33 (my translation).

[76] See Racine, "Les formes de violence émergeant de la mondialisation," in Noël (Ed.), *Mondialisation, violence et religion*, pp. 33-44.

[77] As I mentioned in the previous chapter above, Monique Dumais documents well the sexual exploitation of women. Here, I refer to her critique of this exploitation within the paradigm of globalization (see "Voies de salut pour les femmes dans le contexte de la violence mondialisée," in Noël [Ed.], *Mondialisation, violence et religion*, pp. 79-80). In another publication, she analyzes the ways in which globalization affects women differently than it does men and, at the same time, how women are implicated directly in these processes (see *Femmes et mondialisation*, Montréal: Médiaspaul [Interpellations], 2009).

[78] Racine, "Les formes de violence émergeant de la mondialisation," in Noël (Ed.), *Mondialisation, violence et religion*, p. 36 (my translation); see also Michel Beaudin, "Le dieu Marché et son culte," in *Relations*, 744 (2010), pp. 27-28. For Beaudin, too, as for Racine, the globalization of the market transforms it into a "god." The market has been idolized, and people are sacrificed in order to obtain its favors. Thus, the market has been transformed into a religion.

products. According to Racine, "[t]he ideological position of the United States, the real political promoter of globalization, is increasingly explicit in this direction."[79] The destruction of particular cultures, religions and national autonomies through the "uniformization of the world" is one of the potential reasons for terrorism and the violent reaction of terrorists to it.[80] The danger of terrorist retaliation emerges when people feel excluded and not recognized for their distinctiveness.

The third form of violence is the "absolutizing of power."[81] I have spoken of the danger of the tendency to use all kinds of military power to impose the views of one nation on another.[82] In the second chapter above, I referred to the belief, espoused by some people and some nations, especially the United States, that they are "chosen by God" to save others from the perceived threat of terrorist enemies.[83]

Finally, the fourth form of violence Racine identifies and reflects on consists in the "exploitation of nature and its resources." I dealt with the violence against nature and its negative consequences in the previous chapter above, where I discussed the "ecological holocaust" and "environmental scarcity." There I explained how these contribute to a spiral of violence.

Yet, Racine is not the only one who discusses and deals with the negative consequences of globalization and its relationship to violence. Various thinkers have helped us see that violence against the poor and the excluded can become a source of more violence. For example, poor and excluded countries retaliate against those they considered to be their oppressors. In many cases, Western countries and, in particular the United States, are pinpointed as oppressive nations.[84] John H. Cobb, Jr., highlights:

[79] Racine, "Les formes de violence émergeant de la mondialisation," in Noël (Ed.), *Mondialisation, violence et religion*, p. 38 (my translation); see also Northcott, *An Angel Directs the Storm*, pp. 21-31, 73-87.

[80] See McTernan, *Violence in God's Name*, pp. 21-22.

[81] See Díez de Velasco, "Theoretical Reflections on Violence and Religion," p. 97.

[82] See, for example, Peter W. Singer, *Wired for War: The Robotics Revolution and Conflict in the Twenty-first Century*, New York: Penguin Books (Technology/Science), 2010 (©2009).

[83] See Tite, "Sacred Violence and the Scholar of Religion as Public Intellectual," in Rennie and Tite (Eds.), *Religion, Terror and Violence*, p. 4.

[84] This is the position of Mark Juergensmeyer: "Activists such as bin Laden," he says, "might be regarded as guerilla antiglobalists. Even local ethnonationalist struggles, such as in Kashmir, have arisen in part because of an erosion of confidence in Western-style politics and politicians. The era of globalization and postmodernity creates a context in which authority is undercut and local forces have been unleashed. In saying this, I do not mean to imply that only globalization causes religious violence. But it may be one reason why so many instances of religious violence in such diverse places around the world are occurring at the present time" (*Terror in the Mind of God*, p. xii;

> The economic policies that drive millions of people off their land and out of their traditional villages are violent ones. They are analogous to the enclosure movement that drove peasants off their land in the eighteenth century. They produce a large pool of unemployed people desperate for work, who will accept almost any pay and conditions.[85]

Given these realities of exclusion and oppression, it is easy to understand why some Islamic terrorist actions carried out by Muslim extremists are rooted in this "ideological conception" of globalization. Many of these extremists feel humiliated, ashamed, and frustrated when they realize how their cultural, political and religious identities[86] are threatened by a Western "pan-culture" and a neoliberal economy, which these extremists perceived to be imposed upon them with the resulting destruction of their own way of life.

5. Culture of Violence, Destruction, and Death

In the second chapter above, I mentioned that, according to Walter Wink[87] and Jack Nelson-Pallmeyer,[88] violence has been transformed into a religion that brings salvation, a religion through which people think they can obtain their ultimate needs and desires. Violence is understood either as "security," "victory," or "revenge." I also cited Chris Hedges, a war journalist who has covered many armed conflicts in different part of the world. He describes how war often becomes an

see also pp. 178-182). As Díez de Velasco points out clearly, "[p]rivilege generates violence in two directions: the violence exerted by the privileged and the violence exerted by those who are not privileged and who desire to become so or who respond to the violence exerted by the former" ("Theoretical Reflections on Violence and Religion," p. 100).

[85] John H. Cobb, Jr., "Economic Aspect of Social and Environmental Violence," p. 6; see also p. 7; Sulak Siviraksa, "Economic Aspects of Social and Environmental Violence from a Buddhist Perspective," in *Buddhist-Christian Studies*, 22 (2002), p. 47.

[86] Joel S. Fetzer and J. Christopher Soper underscore the risk of imposing a "majority religion." This imposition can become a source of violence on the part of the "minorities" who do not feel respected in their own faith. "The majority religion," they say, "often with the support of the state, subjects minority religions to various types of social and political discrimination. Minority groups respond by forming movements of religious defense, thereby bringing religious cleavages to the center of partisanship and political debate" ("The Roots of Public Attitudes toward State Accommodation of European Muslims' Religious Practices Before and After September 11," in Rennie and Tite [Eds.], *Religion, Terror and Violence*, p. 163).

[87] See Wink, *Engaging the Powers*, p. 3; Wink, *The Power That Be*, pp. 37-62.

[88] See Nelson-Pallmeyer, *Is Religion Killing Us?*, p. 136.

entertainment. It becomes a distraction and keeps people amused.[89] For this reason, and following in a sense Marx's critique of religion as the "opium of the people," I considered violence as a "new opium" for dealing with painful experiences.

Linked to this understanding of violence as religion, J. Harold Ellens shows how an "apocalyptic vision of the world," very present in today's cultures, is rooted in religious visions that support a metaphysical and dualistic conception of the world locked into a global, transcendent, battle between "good" and "evil." According to him,

> [a]pocalyptic evangelists, film producers, arcade machine purveyors, designers of the violent Disney videos, and those Fundamentalist Islamic terrorists are all in the same category in terms of the unconscious metaphors by which they are shaped, to which they appeal, and that they constantly reinforce in our cultures. Moreover, the Master Story from which they derive their unconscious metaphors is the tradition of Western religions: Judaism, Christianity, and Islam. The Western world will need to decide whether it wishes to change this destructive story and its vicious core metaphors, or continue to wreak increasing psychospiritual havoc upon itself until the metaphor becomes so pervasive that we will all feel relieved with the impending prospect of a final cataclysmic Armageddon, closing out history.[90]

Yet, it is not necessary to formulate extreme positions or to carry out subtle analyses in order to recognize the omnipresence of an "all-powerful" violence in our culture. There are three rather more direct and simple activities that I frequently use in my courses, particularly when I speak of our participation in and solidarity with the "sin of the world" which can help us understand the reality of violence in our culture. The first of these three activities is a group activity. It consists in preparing a blank poster and pasting it to the wall. Then, I distribute different newspapers to students, asking them to identify the headlines that touch them, cut them out, and then paste them onto the blank poster. When everyone has finished, we analyze the content of the headlines as a class. What a spectacle! Murders, rapes, wars, crimes, robberies, and the like are the more frequent choices made by the students.

The second activity can be done more individually and alone. Students are instructed to sit down and watch the news on television or to

[89] See Hedges, *War Is a Force that Gives Us Meaning*, pp. 9, 98-99.

[90] Ellens, "Introduction," in Ellens (Ed.), *The Destructive Power of Religion*, vol. 1, p. 5.

listen to it on the radio. At the end of watching or listening to the news, the students are asked to count how many "good" news pieces they saw or listened to. As in the previous exercise, the results can be very depressing. I would not be surprised to learn of population polls showing that fewer people watch or listen to the news because of the violence that is constantly portrayed in such programs.

Finally, the third activity which can help us recognize the omnipresence of violence in our culture consists of just sitting down and watching movies or at least parts of movies on television, whether alone or with others. The purpose of the exercise is to count how many movies have the following note, or some variations of it: "This program contains scenes of violence, coarse language, and nudity. Viewer discretion is advised." The number of these programs on television is troubling. Violence, in all its forms, has become a spectacle that, progressively, makes people become desensitized to it. It is almost as if people have become violence "junkies," dependent on violence for their "fix," their entertainment. As J. Harold Ellens points out, violence has become an addiction, particularly for young people:

> Moreover, one need only stop for a half hour in any game machine arcade in the Americas or Europe, Japan or Australia, South Africa or any other culture influenced by Western social values, to notice the glassy-eyed addiction of young people to acting out symbolic murder scenes and extermination of entire groups of persons, as well as massive property structures, in the most extreme forms of violence in the virtual reality of those machines. One can see and hear the offensive animalist gestures and sounds of glee and satisfaction expressed by these young people as they create, in that virtual world, the abuse, destruction, conflagrations, and termination of people and things for which some dark archetype in their infected souls longs.[91]

In short, violence, with the intentional causing of death as its ultimate manifestation, has been transformed into a spectacle to be watched, an entertainment and a distraction. The problem is, interestingly, that it is always perceived as something that happens to others and not to oneself. The violence that is unfortunately very much present in our culture diminishes the overall meaning of death as such. Attitudes like these

[91] J. Harold Ellens, "Introduction: The Interface of Religion, Psychology, and Violence," in Ellens (Ed.), *The Destructive Power of Religion*, vol. 2, pp. 7-8; see also Wink, "The Myth of Redemptive Violence," in Ellens (Ed.), *The Destructive Power of Religion*, vol. 3, pp. 269-276.

contribute to a tendency to avoid asking serious questions about the ultimate, even metaphysical meaning of death.[92] Death and dying are for other people. We are only spectators!

Considering how much violence is present during childhood and adolescence, either through domestic violence, on television, in video-games, movies, comics, and so forth, it is not surprising to see how much this violence affects children's development.[93] As a society, we should not be surprised if this saturation of violence produces perverse effects in the long term.[94] In a particular way, as I have presented in the third chapter above, experiences of violence during childhood risk making children, who are spectators of such violence, into perpetrators of it themselves.

* * *

In this chapter, I presented five approaches for understanding violence and what gives rise to it. These approaches help us see that violence emerges within many different contexts. Violence is present within the Holy Scriptures of the three monotheistic religions, where Yahweh, Jesus Christ and Allah would seem to justify violent acts. Violence is further concretized as often being rooted in patriarchy, which is in effect the socio-politico and cultural substratum underlying what one can call toxic sacred texts. Violence is one of the causes of the humiliation and shame that many people experience and which generate negative emotions such as anger and hate. When violence is seen as being one of the consequences of the "ideological conception" of globalization, with its denial of diversity and the oppression of the poor and as being at the center of a culture of destruction and death, it seems to be everywhere and, dare we say, rather all-pervasive.

[92] See Joseph Ratzinger [Pope Benedict XVI], *Eschatology: Death and Eternal Life* (M. Waldestein, trans.), Washington: Catholic University of America Press (Dogmatic Theology, 9), 1988, pp. 70-71; Johann Hofmeier, "The Present-Day Experience of Death," in *Concilium*, 4/10 (1974), pp. 19-23.

[93] The consequences of violence in the development of children have been extensively studied. Taking into account the importance of "mirroring," that is, to take others as models, particularly those that are "important ones" in our lives, or "famous ones" that we desire to emulate, we can understand how negative the influence of violent programs can be, especially on children (see Gormly and Brodzinsky, *Lifespan Human Development*, pp. 298-302).

[94] See Wink, "The Myth of Redemptive Violence," in Ellens (Ed,), *The Destructive Power of Religion*, vol. 3, pp. 276-278.

Thus, we can draw a fourth conclusion about violence, namely, that perpetrators of violence are also themselves victims of it. In a culture of violence, they are victims of the violence inflicted upon them, or victims of their own distorted and, oftentimes, pathological personalities and behaviors, or both. To recognize this multifaceted reality of being a victim of violence leads us to the need to accept, in one way or another, our personal responsibility and, particularly, our social responsibility in overcoming violence. As Helena Cobban says:

> In the West we like to make simplistic, though judgment-laden, distinctions between "victims" or "survivors" of violent acts and "perpetrators." We tend to ignore the traumatization that perpetrators suffer; we ignore, also, the fact that many "victims/survivors" are not themselves pure innocents; indeed, frequently people who have themselves survived the torment of others go on to become enactors of torment in their turn. We like to put people in strict, dyadical boxes, and we expect them to stay there. Real-life instances of atrocious violence are seldom like that, however, a fact that Primo Levi ["The Gray Zone"] has explored possibly better than anyone else.[95]

What Helena Cobban highlights here is in line with what I have previously indicated: there is always a temptation to demonize enemies in order to justify our own violence against them. Yet, it is very difficult to recognize the enemy within oneself, or in ourselves as a society. It is even more difficult to realize that we are "saved by the enemy" as was discussed in the first chapter above.[96] In other words, we have to look at enemies from a wider perspective with "God's eyes." This is why we need a personal, as well as a socio-political conversion, to move away from violence to peace.

[95] Helena Cobban, "Religion and Violence," in *Journal of the American Academy of Religion*, 73/4 (2005), p. 1136.

[96] See Redekop, *From Violence to Blessing*, p. 29; Wink, *The Powers That Be*, pp. 170-171; Nelson-Pallmeyer, *Is Religion Killing Us?*, p. 126.

Chapter 5

Re-Envisioning Religion and Culture

Is it possible to overcome violence? Is it possible to build a culture of peace and re-envision religion accordingly? There is no doubt that, even if we were not successful in eliminating all sources of violence, as scholars and practitioners of religion we are called to find solutions permitting us to come to terms with those sources that can be identified.

In this chapter, I will deal with the ways in which different sources of violence, as identified in the previous chapter, can be recast and transformed to enable us to foster peace. I will in effect explore the relationship between religion and culture not from the perspective of and in line with a paradigm of violence but, rather, from a concern for, and according to, a paradigm of peace. First, I will question the inadequate way in which God has been considered the true author of the Holy Scriptures. Second, taking into consideration how patriarchy continues to distort the relationship between men and women, as well as between humanity and creation as a whole, I will suggest a move to bring about gender equality. Third, I will focus on the importance of healing the wounds of violence, particularly those brought about through humiliation and the engendering of shame. This healing must not only be personal but also communal, since violence is the result not only of individual acts but, importantly, of socio-political, economic and environmental injustices. There is a crying need to address these injustices to avoid the generation of further humiliation and shame. Fourth, and as a counterpart to the "ideological conception" of globalization, I will speak of its "utopian conception," namely, how, when understood positively, globalization can be an instrument of social justice as well as economic, environmental and religious solidarity. Fifth, I will underline the importance of remembering and truth, that is to say, recalling the events that have wounded people and revealing the truth about what really happened in order for all concerned to enter into processes of reconciliation. This itinerary needs to be accompanied by the willingness to listen to victims' voices. Finally, I will reflect on what it means for us to understand the relationship between religion and culture out of a paradigm of, and concern for, peace.

1. Questioning the Divine Authorship of Holy Scriptures

In the first part of the previous chapter, I addressed the problem of the violence expressed and seemingly encouraged in many of the sacred texts of the three monotheistic religions. I presented these texts as a means through which we can understand violent behavior. As we saw, understanding violence, and here we mean of course especially violence arising in one way or another out of religion, involves not only the fact that we are dealing with the question of a literal, selective, and fundamentalist interpretation of Holy Scriptures. It also requires recognizing the fact that a number of these texts presuppose and often directly present the image of a "warrior," even "pathological," God. Therefore, understanding violence and its relationship to religion requires that we grapple with the conviction many believers have within these three religions that their Holy Scriptures have God as their true author or that they have been directly revealed by God to some special people. Jack Nelson-Pallmeyer considers this overall conviction to be at the root of much violent behavior. This is also the position of many other scholars, to some of whom I will make reference in the following section below.

The question that I would like to address here is: How can God be conceived as the true author of the Holy Scriptures of the three monotheistic religions? I will answer this question in three steps. First, I will deal with the position of some scholars who address this important point from different perspectives in biblical and Qur'anic hermeneutics. Second, I will consider what I believe to be the most important aspect of dealing with the question of God as the true author of the Holy Scriptures, namely, the catechetical and pastoral applications of the results of biblical and Qur'anic hermeneutics on this issue. Once again, it will be important to take into consideration the fact that believers are generally not scholars trained in the various disciplines involved in the more scholarly and scientific study of Holy Scriptures. Yet, the question of Divine authorship of these Scriptures should not and cannot be left to experts alone. Such an approach would simply allow for an uncritical use of the idea of God as the true author of Scriptures in catechesis and pastoral practices in general and would make it practically impossible for us truly to come to terms with "pathological" notions of God. Third, and finally, I will summarize my own position on this issue.

From Biblical and Qur'anic Hermeneutical Perspectives

In the first chapter above, I referred to the need to deconstruct "the pathological portraits of God" (Jack Nelson-Pallmeyer), the presentation of a "perverse God" (Maurice Bellet) and, the element or aspect, of violence on the part of Jesus Christ presented in the New Testament (J. Harold Ellens). This deconstruction was the principal intention of the authors alluded to shortly above: to liberate the Divine from the image of a warrior and cruel God, the God of terror into which Yahweh was converted. From the image of an almost pathological God, of a God who seemingly almost cruelly watches and judges all, we need to move toward an image of a compassionate and merciful God, as it is revealed in the core message of Jesus Christ. To deconstruct such toxic texts, these authors challenge the traditional conception of God as the true author of the Holy Scriptures, at least in so far as God would be considered the direct author of texts that carry on this pathological portrait of God! Unfortunately, this topic remains taboo for many religious leaders within Judaism, Christianity, and Islam. "The cruelty of God," says Nelson-Pallmeyer, "is a problem that almost no one is willing to face squarely, including Christian interpreters."[1] However, today the task of confronting God's "cruelty" is urgent given the reality of terrorist actions perpetrated in God's name.

According to Nelson-Pallmeyer, it is necessary to make an important distinction between "revelation" and "distortion."[2] He writes that not only Christianity as such but also the evangelists themselves "went away" from the true message of Jesus Christ. "[T]he New Testament writers," says Nelson-Pallmeyer, "betray Jesus because they interpret the meaning of his life, death, and resurrection in light of violent images of God and expectations of history that Jesus himself rejected."[3] For this reason, there is a need to recover the "lost Jesus," and the non-violent images of God that Jesus reveals. In fact, it is not possible to separate the Christ of faith from the historical Jesus without falling into the ideology and the idolatry of a Gnostic Christ.

Thus, the main purpose of Nelson-Pallmeyer's work is to demonstrate that the God of Jesus of Nazareth, the God Jesus presents out of his own experience, is not pathological. On the contrary, the God of

[1] Nelson-Pallmeyer, *Jesus against Christianity*, p. 21.
[2] See Nelson-Pallmeyer, *Jesus against Christianity*, pp. 65, 154.
[3] Nelson-Pallmeyer, *Is Religion Killing Us?*, p. 59.

Jesus is opposed to any religious justification of violence.[4] In order to provide a different, non-violent image of God, Nelson-Pallmeyer analyzes contradictions found in the Gospels. This analysis can be extended to the other writings of the New Testament and to imperial Christianity as well in order to discern more clearly "the meaning of Jesus' life and death."[5] In fact, he states, "[o]ur embrace of imperial Christianity distorts the content and substance of Christian faith sufficiently enough to constitute a betrayal of Jesus."[6] Jesus "exposed" the "violence and exploitation" of the unjust socio-political, economic and religious structures of his time.[7] The God of Jesus is a God of compassion, love, justice, solidarity and forgiveness; all of these are essential elements in any successful overcoming of the spiral of violence.[8] The problem, then, is not with religion as such, which for Nelson-Pallmeyer has profound value as a bearer of meaning, but with the destructive role that toxic sacred texts play in a world fractured by violence, inequality, war, intolerance, and hate. Considering the violent texts of the Bible and of the Qur'an as "sacred" distorts God and faith, and gives religious legitimacy to human violence. Challenging those traditions and texts is an essential act of faithfulness for believers in the twenty-first century.[9]

Nelson-Pallmeyer is not the only scholar questioning what so many have come to consider the traditional conception of God as the true author of the Holy Scriptures. David Wenham, a specialist on Pauline literature, makes the following observation:

[4] As he says, "Jesus' images of God undermine expectations that ultimate justice will be *imposed* by a powerful, violent God. The God revealed through Jesus is not vengeful, violent, judging, or punishing because all of these attributes are foreign to God's nature. Jesus' God, quite simply, is not powerful, at least not in the ways human beings have associated power with violence and then projected that power onto God. The nonviolent power of God is not coercive because God's power is invitational and is not backed by punishing sanctions. God, according to Jesus, is the all-encompassing Spirit that embraces us everywhere and always. This Spirit calls us to new life here and now.... The Spirit is infinitely giving, loving, compassionate, and forgiving. We cannot imagine or accept such a gracious God, and so violence spirals out of control, and the abundant life of the 'invitational kingdom' exists in the shadows of our lives just beyond our reach" (Nelson-Pallmeyer, *Jesus against Christianity*, p. 289).

[5] Nelson-Pallmeyer, *Jesus against Christianity*, p. 154; see also pp. 159-165, where he describes his methodological approach to rediscover the historical Jesus.

[6] Nelson-Pallmeyer, *Jesus against Christianity*, p. 169; see also his book *Is Religion Killing Us?*, pp. 145-146.

[7] See Nelson-Pallmeyer, *Jesus against Christianity*, p. 279.

[8] See Nelson-Pallmeyer, *Jesus against Christianity*, p. 284.

[9] See Nelson-Pallmeyer, *Is Religion Killing Us?*, p. xvi.

> The traditional Christian view of Scripture as a book that speaks with one voice–God's voice–has been vigorously challenged in recent years. Scripture speaks with many voices, it is said–many different *human* voices, saying significantly different things. The diversity is such that, in the view of many, we cannot speak of *the* theology of the Bible, or even of *the* theology of the NT, since there are different, even contradictory, theologies in the two Testaments. Whether we can continue to speak of the unity of Scripture or even to regard the Bible as the inspired word of God is debated among scholars, with most agreeing that old definitions of the unity and inspiration of the Bible need to be replaced.[10]

From a Catholic perspective, this issue has also been addressed in an indirect way by the Twelfth Ordinary General Assembly of the Synod of Bishops (Vatican City, October 5-26, 2008). In the "working document" (*Instrumentum Laboris*) sent to the participants, and in relationship with what I have been presenting here, there are several important points we should note and underline.[11]

The first is the recognition that at the core of the word of God, taken in its various senses, there is Jesus Christ. He is the light by and through which we understand the word of God.[12]

The second important point is the recognition that the word of God, without denying its relationship to the Holy Scriptures and divine inspiration, is more than the written texts of the Bible. The word of God is present in the heart of the ecclesial community, the Church. Without this essential and dynamic relationship to the word of God, the Holy Scriptures risk being interpreted in a subjectivist and fundamentalist way.[13] The "working document" also acknowledges the existence of "ideological" conceptions of the Bible that consider it to be just a human enterprise. Yet, there is a real difference between considering the Bible "simply as human words apart from faith"[14] and seeing it as the "human expression" of the encounter with God.

[10] David Wenham, *Paul: Follower of Jesus or Founder of Christianity?*, Grand Rapids, Cambridge (UK): William B. Eerdmans Publishing Co. 1995, p. 12.

[11] See Synod of Bishops, *The Word of God in the Life and Mission of the Church* (*Instrumentum Laboris*), at http://www.vatican.va/roman_curia/synod/documents/rc_synod_doc_20080511_instrlabor-xii-assembly_en.html (accessed September 28, 2011).

[12] See Synod of Bishops, *The Word of God in the Life and Mission of the Church* (*Instrumentum Laboris*), Part I, Chapter 1, number 11.

[13] See Synod of Bishops, *The Word of God in the Life and Mission of the Church* (*Instrumentum Laboris*), Part I, Chapter 2, numbers 14-15, 19-22.

[14] Synod of Bishops, *The Word of God in the Life and Mission of the Church* (*Instrumentum Laboris*), Part I, Chapter 2, number 20.

In a similar vein, on November 11, 2010, two years after the end of the Synod of Bishops, Pope Benedict XVI published the traditional Post-Synodal Apostolic Exhortation on the matter.[15] The style and the content of a pontifical document are very different from a "working document." Nevertheless, as was the case for the "working document" of the Synod, the Post-Synodal Apostolic Exhortation draws attention to nuances between the written text of the Bible and the word of God, which is more inclusive: "All this helps us to see," says Benedict XVI, "that, while in the Church we greatly venerate the sacred Scriptures, the Christian faith is not a 'religion of the book',... Consequently the Scripture is to be proclaimed, heard, read, received and experienced as the word of God, in the stream of the apostolic Tradition from which it is inseparable."[16]

The Post-Synodal Apostolic Exhortation refers as well to the "dark" passages of the Bible. However, the document deals with them in a confusing and limited way, while taking into account the gravity of the problem of toxic sacred texts. Benedict XVI points out how revelation is rooted in history, unfolds slowly, and progressively against human resistance, recognizing that all of this can disturb the modern reader. Yet, quite unexpectedly we read at the end of the same passage:

> So it would be a mistake to neglect those passages of Scripture that strike us as problematic. Rather, we should be aware that the correct interpretation of these passages requires a degree of expertise, acquired through a training that interprets the texts in their historical-literary context and within the Christian perspective which has as its ultimate hermeneutical key [the new commandment of love of Jesus Christ]. I encourage scholars and pastors to help all faithful to approach these

[15] See Pope Benedict XVI, *The Word of God in the Life and Mission of the Church (Verbum Domini)*, at http://www.vatican.va/holy_father/benedict_xvi/apost_exhortations/documents/hf_ben-xvi_exh_20100930_verbum-domini_en.pdf (accessed September 28, 2011).

[16] Benedict XVI, *The Word of God in the Life and Mission of the Church (Verbum Domini)*, number 7. The Pope referred to the Synod Fathers who used the image of a symphony for speaking on the different ways of interpreting the expression of the "word of God": "As the Synod Fathers stated," says Benedict XVI, "the expression 'word of God' is used analogically, and we should be aware of this. The faithful need to be better helped to grasp the different meanings of the expression, but also to understand its unitary sense. From the theological standpoint too, there is a need for further study of how the different meanings of this expression are interrelated, so that the unity of God's plan and, within it, the centrality of the person of Christ, may shine forth more clearly" (number 7; see also André Paul, "Pourquoi une communauté se dote-t-elle d'un canon?," in *Le Monde de la Bible*, 196 [2011], p. 18).

> passages through an interpretation which enables their meaning to emerge in the light of the mystery of Christ.[17]

Benedict XVI also deals with the risk of fundamentalist approaches to the Bible. Here, the document passes very quickly and in a puzzling way over the urgent problem of interpretation. According to the Pope, "[t]he 'literalism' championed by the fundamentalist approach actually represents a betrayal of both the literal and the spiritual sense, and opens the way to various forms of manipulation, as, for example, by disseminating anti-ecclesial interpretations of the Scriptures."[18] I believe that the problem with fundamentalist approaches goes beyond the risk of "disseminating anti-ecclesial interpretations of Scriptures." As mentioned in the previous chapter above, these approaches can be considered "religious ideologies" which have wide-ranging implications, especially for any consideration of religion in relation to violence

For Benedict XVI, there is no doubt that the "primary setting" for biblical hermeneutics is the Church.[19] Within these parameters, the most important principle of interpretation, from the perspective of the Pope, that is, "the directive to be considered appropriate in hermeneutics," is the Dogmatic Constitution on Divine Revelation (*Dei Verbum*) of the Second Vatican Council (1962–1965).[20] For Benedict XVI, using the principles of this document as a guide is the way to avoid "the danger of dualism" between exegetical (scientific) and theological (more faith-related) approaches to Holy Scriptures. Benedict XVI, together with the Synod of Bishops, also underscores the risk of falling into "a secularized hermeneutic," namely, an "ideological hermeneutics" that does not recognize any Divine intervention in history.[21]

Even after reference to these two Roman Catholic documents, namely, the Post-Synodal Apostolic Exhortation on the Word of God and the Dogmatic Constitution on Divine Revelation of the Second Vatican Council, in the end the same questions remain: Are human beings the

[17] Benedict XVI, *The Word of God in the Life and Mission of the Church (Verbum Domini)*, number 42.

[18] Benedict XVI, *The Word of God in the Life and Mission of the Church (Verbum Domini)*, number 44.

[19] See Benedict XVI, *The Word of God in the Life and Mission of the Church (Verbum Domini)*, number 29.

[20] See Benedict XVI, *The Word of God in the Life and Mission of the Church (Verbum Domini)*, number 34.

[21] See Benedict XVI, *The Word of God in the Life and Mission of the Church (Verbum Domini)*, number 35.

divinely inspired authors of these "dark" passages and God the true author of them? Is not this distinction confusing and even perhaps ideological? Can we say, in a liturgical proclamation at the end of the reading of these toxic sacred texts: "the word of God"? The Post-Synodal Apostolic Exhortation lamentably seems to pass over the real problem that I have been dealing with in this book. It is unfortunate that Benedict XVI passes so quickly over what he calls "dark" texts and the fundamentalist tendencies of contemporary approaches to the Holy Scriptures and religiosity in general. This issue is particularly important when considered in the context of contemporary religiously motivated terrorism. It is certain that Benedict XVI does not share David Wenham's opinions regarding the need for reinterpreting and replacing the "old definitions of the unity and inspiration of the Bible."[22] As I mentioned before, questioning the traditional conception of God as the true author of the Holy Scriptures is taboo among many religious leaders in the three monotheistic religions.

Despite recognizing that the Post-Synodal Apostolic Exhortation of Benedict XVI tries to contribute to a biblical renewal within the Roman Catholic Church, and acknowledging that there are many positive points in this document, we may well find surprising to read the following remark at the beginning of the document. Speaking on "Sacred Scripture, inspiration and truth," the Pope writes: "In this way one recognizes the full importance of the human author who wrote the inspired texts and, at the same time, God himself as the true author."[23] Benedict XVI, in spite of briefly addressing the "dark" texts of Holy Scriptures and the risks of fundamentalist interpretations, spends little time on this issue. Sadly, these points were not considered at greater length when we recognize the existence of so much contemporary violence perpetrated in God's name!

For his part, Hans Küng extends the question of God as the true author of the Holy Scriptures to the Qur'an. According to him, there is a need to take into account the fact that the Qur'an "... descended into the Prophet's 'heart', was proclaimed by him and only then written down and collected together. Even orthodox Islamic Qur'anic scholarship has never disguised the fact that the holy book as we have it today was written decades after the death of the Prophet."[24] As a result of Küng's discus-

[22] Wenham, *Paul*, p. 12.

[23] Benedict XVI, *The Word of God in the Life and Mission of the Church (Verbum Domini)*, number 19.

[24] Küng, *Islam*, p. 67; see also pp. 68, 268. In fact, later on, Küng asks the question regarding the need to have a kind of Qur'anic criticism, as is the case with biblical criticism (see pp. 518-521).

sion on the need for a Qur'anic criticism, similar to that carried out concerning the Hebrew Scriptures and the New Testament, he states:

> The Qur'an should not be understood, any more than the Bible should be, as a system of fixed formulae, rigid doctrines, unchangeable legal principles, as if it could be handed down unhistorically with no heed to time, place and persons. History cannot be dispensed with. Anything else would be an uncritical dogmatic understanding of the Qur'an–whether with a Muslim or a Christian stamp.[25]

In conclusion, we must recognize more directly and openly the three monotheistic religions' need to confront the presence of violence within their sacred texts. Nelson-Pallmeyer is certainly one of those who has approached this issue more directly. He writes, "[d]oubting the authority of 'sacred texts' that legitimate violence is an essential act of faithfulness."[26] The encouragement of violence, within the three monotheistic religions, is the result of refusing "to fully challenge the authority of 'sacred texts' that overflow with violent images of God and stories justifying human violence in God's name." [27]

These toxic texts are the result of patriarchy, and a way of projecting onto God human pathological desires. This is something which has even entered into the liturgical prayer and into other forms of religious worshiping. Thus, according to Nelson-Pallmeyer, "[p]urging Christianity of violent images of God would also force Christians to take nonviolent power and the radical nonviolence of Jesus seriously, something few seem willing to do."[28] A few pages later, he continues with the same argument:

> Jews, Christians, and Muslims must address the problem of violence and "sacred" text if we are to have any reasonable hope for an alternative future. A world being destroyed by violence, much of it done with justifying reference to God and "sacred" text, is a world in desperate need of new understandings of divine and human power. The futility of violence and resiliency of injustice requires us to unleash our imaginations in order to move beyond religious certainties into unfamiliar terrain where patriarchal assumptions that dominate "sacred" texts and political life are challenged in light of historical need and human experience.[29]

[25] Küng, *Islam*, pp. 533-534; see also Mooren, *War and Peace in Monotheistic Religions*, p. 153; Thomas Mooren, "September 11th 2001 and the Future of Monotheistic Religions," in *MST Review*, 6/1 (2004), pp. 38-72.

[26] Nelson-Pallmeyer, *Is Religion Killing Us?*, p. 96.

[27] Nelson-Pallmeyer, *Is Religion Killing Us?*, p. 98.

[28] Nelson-Pallmeyer, *Is Religion Killing Us?*, p. 98.

[29] Nelson-Pallmeyer, *Is Religion Killing Us?*, p. 108.

Is then God the true author of the Holy Scriptures within the three monotheistic religions? Nelson-Pallmeyer suggests that Jews, Christians, and Muslins, have to ask themselves this essential question. Why do they not recognize that the Bible and the Qur'an are the work of human beings who put their religious experiences in writing, namely, the way in which they see history from a religious perspective?[30] He develops what I feel is the core of his position in the following passage. It is worth quoting in full:

> Accepting human authorship of the Bible and the Quran and the inevitable distortions of God that accompany all human efforts to interpret human experience as religious experience would open up many possibilities. It would allow us to see the legacy of abusive men's power in the Bible and Quran, including how male conceptions of punishing, coercive violence are projected onto God and used to justify human violence against women and outsiders. This could be a basis to reflect on similar dynamics at play in our world, where men, violence, and religion are links in a strong chain holding the world captive to violence. We could examine explanations for historical catastrophes, expectations of God's power, and justifications for human violence in the Bible and the Quran in light of present injustices and similarly distorted views of history, violence, and power today.
>
> The problem with this alternative approach or way of reading "sacred" texts is that it is unthinkable for many Jews and Christians and would be considered scandalous by many Muslims. It seems to me, however, that whatever method or pathway Jews, Christians, and Muslims choose, they must effectively challenge the violence-of-God traditions at the heart of the Bible and the Quran. Doing so is an essential component of faithfulness as we seek to create an alternative future consistent with God's compassion.[31]

I fully agree with Nelson-Pallmeyer in recognizing that religious experience is always the "human experience of the divine."[32] It is the person, with all her particularities and specific traits of personality, who experiences and expresses her encounter with God. The religious dimension of the experience is, then, inserted into human experience as such. In this regard, the *chiaroscuro* of every "human experience of the Divine" becomes important for scriptural criticism. This obliges believers to enter

[30] See Nelson-Pallmeyer, *Is Religion Killing Us?*, pp. 134-135.

[31] Nelson-Pallmeyer, *Is Religion Killing Us?*, p. 135.

[32] I am referring here to the French title of the book by Michel Meslin, *L'expérience humaine du divin: Fondements d'une anthropologie religieuse*, Paris: Éditions du Cerf (Cogitatio Fidei, 150), 1988.

into a process of continual discernment to discover the divine dimension when it is present in a human experience and to avoid its distortion.[33]

From Catechetical and Pastoral Points of View

The question of scriptural criticism, that is, of biblical and Qur'anic hermeneutics, is then an essential task in overcoming the problem of sacred toxic texts and their serving as a source giving rise to various forms of individual and social violence. Yet, this is not a problem only for biblical and Qur'anic scholars. It needs to be addressed from a catechetical and pastoral point of view as well. There is a moral obligation for Christian church authorities, and for religious leaders within Judaism and Islam, to address the problem of toxic sacred texts within catechesis and liturgical celebration at large.

As previously noted, the Pope reminds scholars and Church leaders: "I encourage scholars and pastors to help all faithful to approach these passages through an interpretation which enables their meaning to emerge in the light of the mystery of Christ."[34] This task is not only a question of giving all sorts of "hermeneutical" explanations for these texts. The most pressing question is: Is God the true author of these "dark" texts? Has God, yes or no, "inspired" those who distort God's intentions? Is the written expression of a "distorted divine word" still a "word of God"? Can believers proclaim at the end of the reading of some of these "dark" texts: "the word of God"? I am deeply convinced that until we deal with the question of the authorship of the Holy Scriptures in a profound way, without underlying ideological presuppositions, we are not going to solve the problem of the "pathological portraits of God."

The three monotheistic religions are founded on the presumption that God, in spite of all the nuances made in this regard, is the true author of the Holy Scriptures. The Bible, then, as the Qur'an, is a "deposit" that also contains God's word. However, it is not always the living God of Abraham, Isaac and Jacob, of Jesus Christ, and of the prophet Muhammad, who continues to speak to us today. Religious leaders, past and present, can be tempted to portray themselves as the sole interpreters of the word of God, particularly if they consider themselves to be part of a

[33] See Louis Dupré, *The Other Dimension: A Search for the Meaning of Religious Attitudes*, Garden City: Doubleday, 1972, pp. 13-33.

[34] Benedict XVI, *The Word of God in the Life and Mission of the Church (Verbum Domini)*, number 42.

privileged group that has the "divine command" to interpret the Holy Scriptures. A risk often associated with falling into "the triumph of ideology." We might go so far as to say that we need a profoundly renewed understanding of divine inspiration of Holy Scriptures that takes fully into consideration the fundamental importance of catechetical, pastoral, and liturgical proclamation.

Life as the Milieu of God's Revelation

Here, as a contribution to a renewed understanding of divine inspiration, I develop my own proposal regarding the Divine authorship of Holy Scriptures and on hermeneutics. Believers are not passive-receptive beings; nor are they slaves to books or norms. Instead, they are invited to enter into a covenant, a relationship, with a living God. Thus, I completely agree with Benedict XVI when he says that Christian faith is not a "religion of a book" but the existential answer to a God who, in Jesus Christ and through the Holy Spirit, continues to manifest God's love to believers as individuals, as members of a community, the Church, and to all of humanity.

Given that religious experience is the "human experience" of the Divine, and human beings share their encounters of God with others, believers should embark on a continual process of hermeneutics, of interpreting these experiences. This is particularly important in light of the problem presented by toxic sacred texts and in light of the ambiguity regarding the real presence of God in them. Religious experience consists of opening oneself to and accepting a God who comes to us and precedes us in the encounter, a God who has constantly been in search of God's people.

Furthermore, such faith is always kept alive within a liturgical context. For this reason, we can understand the need to renew liturgical celebrations. The people of the First Covenant also celebrated their encounters with God in their liturgies. In fact, most of the biblical texts in the Hebrew Scriptures were born as an expression of the religious experiences that the people of Israel had with the God of their fathers. Before putting these religious encounters in writing, such encounters were celebrated liturgically. Thus, theology has always been a reflection on and arises out of the life of the community.[35]

[35] See Thomas Römer, "Les origines de la Bible hébraïque," in *Le Monde de la Bible*, 196 (2011), pp. 20-25.

This was also true for the Christian communities in the first centuries. It is amazing to realize that these communities, particularly prior to the fourth century and before the end of the persecution of Christians, were able to keep their faith in the God of Jesus Christ alive despite not being able often to gather together publically or to call provincial and ecumenical Councils. It is even more amazing since Christians may not have had an official list or "canon" of the accepted "divinely inspired books" of the Bible until the fourth century.[36] Nonetheless, Christians kept the "orthodoxy" of their faith within the life of their communities and developed it within their liturgical celebrations.

The Bible, even as a holy text, is the written expression of the experiences of God on the part of these communities and of certain other people.[37] Communities and individuals put in writing the ways in which they recognized the God of the Covenant.[38] They did it for themselves, for their celebrations, for missionary purposes, and for sharing their experiences of God with posterity.[39] The written texts are, therefore, like the narratives we develop regarding the stories of our families.

[36] See André Paul, "Le processus de canonisation de l'Ancien Testament," in *Le Monde de la Bible*, 196 (2011), pp. 30-32; Éric Junod, "Le processus de canonisation du Nouveau Testament," in *Le Monde de la Bible*, 196 (2011), pp. 33-35.

[37] As Charles T. Davis III underlines, "[t]he books of the Hebrew Bible (also called 'the Torah, the Prophets, and the Writings,' or TANAK), the Christian Bible, and the Qur'an were not scripture when first written but literary texts. The various books became scripture through their impact upon the life of the community and the process of canonization; consequently, scripture never exists apart from a particular community's interpretation of the texts. Interpretation creates scripture" ("The Qur'an, Muhammad, and Jihad in Context," in Ellens [Ed.], *The Destructive Power of Religion*, vol. 1, p. 234).

[38] "God," as says Peter Schmidt, "reveals himself *through* the testimony of faith of men [and women]. The Bible, from the first to the last word, is the word of man [and woman] and the expression of a human faith conviction" ("Fait historique et vérité théologique," in *Communio*, VII/1 [1982], p. 35 [my translation]). This is also what former Archbishop Desmond Tutu's book, written with Douglas Abrams, highlights: "Reading the Bible can be a source of reflection and inspiration, as you listen for God's voice in your life. But you must watch how you read the Bible and apply it to today's world. The Bible is not something that came dropping from heaven, written by the hand of God. It was written by human beings, so it uses human idiom and is influenced by the context in which whatever story was written. People need to be very careful. Many tend to be literalists, people who believe in the verbal inerrancy of the Bible, who speak as if God dictated the Bible, when in fact God used human beings as they were, and they spoke only as they could speak at that time. There are parts of the Bible that have no permanent worth–that is nothing to be sorry about, it is just to say that it is the Word of God in the words of men and women" (*God Has a Dream: A Vision of Hope for Our Time*, New York, Toronto: Doubleday, 2004, pp. 105-106).

[39] See Paul, "Pourquoi une communauté se dote-t-elle d'un canon?," p. 19.

I remember returning home during holidays. Often, with my sisters, my brother, nephews and nieces, we would share family stories. I still remember the amusement of the children listening to us. Looking back now, I realize that, in fact, we never told the stories twice in the same way. For this reason we were never bored by telling them and listening to them. We always added something new. I cannot say that we were lying, or that we were inventing narratives. We were ourselves simply part of the stories we were telling.

Oftentimes, we are not always sure where stories start and where they will end. The fact is that we are contributing to these family stories with our own experiences, with our own dreams, and so on.[40] Thus, we cannot use our scientific criteria of historicity concerning what is real or not to analyze these family stories. Their certainty belongs at another level. There is no doubt that these stories are true for us! Yet, as in the written expressions of the experiences of God in the Holy Scriptures, sometimes we project, within these family stories, our selfish interests, reshaping them for our own benefit, sometimes out of our own more distorted perceptions of others and even conditioned by or in line with our own pathological personalities. It would seem to me that this is also the way in which the Holy Scriptures were written, and the reason for finding in them so many toxic, "dark" texts.[41]

Additionally, I believe that the Holy Scriptures should not be considered as fully finished, because our "sacred stories" of today are also "the word of God." These are stories in which we recognize God's presence

[40] For John J. Collins, this is also the process through which Israel built up its identity: "It is a commonplace of modern scholarship to say that the books of the Torah and the Deuteronomistic history are engaged in the construction of the identity of 'Israel.' What they reflect is not Israel as it was, but Israel as the authors thought it should be. Identity is defined negatively by a sharp differentiation of Israel from the other peoples of the land and positively by the prescriptions of a covenant with a jealous sovereign God" ("The Zeal of Phinehas, the Bible, and the Legitimation of Violence," in Ellens [Ed.], *The Destructive Power of Religion*, vol. 1, p. 18; see also pp. 17, 23, 25-26).

[41] J. Harold Ellens says the following in this regard: "Stanley Hauerwas urges that we can know no truth but story. Only in telling stories to each other do we distill what is operationally true for us. I would add that what is only abstractly or theoretically true is not true insofar as it is not operational. Thus Hauerwas argues that it is utterly crucial that we take story with the utmost seriousness. As our stories intersect with those of others, both are illumined, and meaning is enlarged. When that other is God, whose story we intersect or whose story may be riding on another person's story, our stories are enlarged supracosmically. When we intersect God's story while realizing our own stories, the enlargement of meaning and illumination has the potential of achieving a transcendental dimension" ("Violence and Christ: God's Crisis and Ours," in Ellens [Ed,], *The Destructive Power of Religion*, vol. 4, p. 188).

among us, even if sometimes we can distort the way in which we perceive and express this presence. I believe, with the deepest respect for the Muslim faithful, that this approach and way of understanding should also be applied to the Qur'an.[42] Consequently, today we are invited to renew our liturgies and our preaching in order that they will be the privileged and sacred times, the divine *kairos*, in which Christian, Jewish, and Muslim communities will be able to celebrate their encounters with God and bear witness to these encounters with others. Thus, in one way or another, we are also invited to continue to write the Holy Scriptures, in communion with what Judeo-Christian, or even Muslim, believers of the past did. We should be attentive to the fact that we are not always able to discern God's true presence in the middle of our lives, particularly when we think that God is for us and against others.

For Christians, the God of Jesus Christ continues to speak to them in the present time. As Benedict XVI highlights so well, Christianity is not a "religion of a book," but faith in the word of God who, in Jesus Christ, became flesh. Therefore, Christian faith is nourished not only by what God wonderfully accomplished in other times, but also by what God, in Jesus Christ and the Holy Spirit, continues to do in our own. As a result, we should be able to put in writing our own experiences of God, in continuity with those experienced by our ancestors in faith and expressed in our Holy Scriptures in order to share them with other communities and to proclaim them with and to all our brothers and sisters. In this regard, we should recognize also the prophets of our own day and have them, or others for them, write down what God has revealed to them in order that they, through their prophetic work, might communicate such revelations to us. Thus, we will have our own book of Job in which to identify those who represent the righteous who have suffered unjustly in our own time. This approach will allow us to choose the love poems we use as we write our own Song of Songs and

[42] I like what Hans Küng says on the Qur'an in this regard: "The Qur'an should be understood, like the Bible, as a living message, repeatedly perceived anew in its recitation as the great prophetic testimony to the one and only powerful and merciful God, the creator and perfecter, his judgment and his promise. It is a completely constant testimony which can and should be handed down in a form that is constantly renewed, varying with time, place and person, so that certain conflicts with nature and history, with modern ethics and awareness of law can be given an unambiguous and constructive solution. That would be a historical-critical-topical understanding with a Muslim or Christian stamp, which takes up the concerns of pluralistic anthropological and political hermeneutics and which does not contradict a believing positive basic attitude to the religion" (*Islam*, p. 534).

identify our own evangelists, those men and women who "have seen," "have touched," and "have been" with the Son of God and will be able to write their Gospels for us today.

Divine inspiration consists in the permanent presence of God's love for us. This presence inspires, in a particular way, certain men and women to tell us of God and God's love for us. Why could official authorities in Christian churches not be able one day to recognize these new writings as inspired? As "canonical" and as rules of faith for believers, just as they once did with the canon of the Bible? From the perspective of the Roman Catholic Church, the last official canon of the Bible was established by the Council of Trent (1545–1563). Accordingly, why is it that the future Church would not be able to recognize other writings as "divinely inspired," namely, as "sacred books," as well?[43] In this sense, I deeply believe that God's revelation to us, today, is a message for peace, a condemnation of all kinds of violence and especially of violence rooted in and arising out of false understandings of religion. This message of peace should be the most important criteria for distinguishing God's presence from our own distortions of the Divine!

I would like to add a further point regarding the need to undertake a hermeneutical interpretation of Holy Scriptures.[44] Hermeneutics is an essential task if we wish to avoid falling into a literal and/or selective interpretation of sacred texts. The function of hermeneutics is to help us interpret the message of the Scriptures in order to actualize them in and for our own time.[45] In this regard, there are three interrelated tasks of hermeneutics.

In the first, hermeneutics provides solutions to problems created by our efforts to express something in differing times and cultures. When faced with historical events or with texts from the past, we are dealing with events or texts belonging to a different cultural context than our own. A hermeneutical approach sensitive to such differences helps us to take such differences into consideration and helps us avoid translating these events or texts literally from one culture or time to another. In other words, we must take into account their socio-cultural and temporal contexts.

The second task of hermeneutics is to assist us in putting events and texts within a larger frame of reference, namely, to situate particular

[43] See Martínez de Pisón, *Life beyond Death*, pp. 98-100; Pierre Gibert, "La suite d'une histoire…," in *Le Monde de la Bible*, 196 (2011), pp. 36-37.

[44] See Martínez de Pisón, *Life beyond Death*, pp. 83-84.

[45] See Gopin, *Between Eden and Armageddon*, pp. 12, 59.

events or texts within the context of their origins, the purpose of the author, and so forth. This is in effect the task of situating the part in relation to the whole. Oftentimes an isolated event or a particular text cannot be understood without its being seen in connection with other circumstances or in relation to other texts. Thus, hermeneutics contributes to finding a greater holistic context within which the part takes on its true significance or fuller meaning.

Finally, as applied to religious language and in particular to theology, hermeneutics helps us to connect the original meaning of an event or text to our present circumstances. Many times the original meaning of an event or text is lost because the context in which this event or text is produced is not taken into account. We must then analyse the frame of reference within which the event or text came to life. To fail to do this type of interpretation is to risk translating the event or text in a far, too literal sense with the risk of then missing the depth of its potential meaning. This is the temptation to which all fundamentalism and dogmatism succumb. The result is often intolerance in the face of diversity and, finally, religious violence.

2. Gender Equality

In our time, feminism as an outlook, attitude and even an overall way of seeing reality represents one of the most significant upheavals in Western culture. It touches all the realms of life–culture, socio-economic and political structures, biblical hermeneutics, religion and, certainly, ecology. The male human being cannot continue to make the rest of created beings subject to his possessive impulses, which are in fact the result of personal insecurity. He has to learn to live in a relationship with women that takes into account their equality and their right to have their own experience of the sacred,[46] and that recognizes the importance of learning how to live in harmony with creation. Learning this is an essential element in moving from patriarchy toward gender equality. In an article published with my colleague, Miriam K. Martin, entitled "From Knowledge to Wisdom,"[47] we challenged

46 See Fran Ferder and John Heagle, "Who Tells the Stories?: Gender and the Experience of the Sacred," in *The Way Supplement*, 92 (1998), pp. 113-123.

47 See Miriam K. Martin and Ramón Martínez de Pisón, "From Knowledge to Wisdom: A New Challenge to the Educational Milieu with Implications for Religious Education," in *Religious Education*, 100/2 (2005), pp. 157-173.

Western epistemological conceptions of the world and, in a particular way, metaphysical presuppositions that advance the theory of the primacy of knowledge and reason, rooted in patriarchy, that have so deeply and negatively affected our understandings of creation, of human beings, and the ways in which learning is acquired. Acknowledging the ways in which these assumptions have affected knowledge, wisdom, and education is part of overcoming the destructive patriarchal and rationalist paradigm of Modernity.

The primary aim in fostering gender equality is to eliminate all kinds of discrimination against women. However, as V. Spike Peterson and Anne Sisson Runyan, two of its pioneering exponents acknowledge, the starting point in achieving gender equality is the recognition of "gender inequality."[48] In their book, they give an excellent definition of gender:

> Unlike **sex** (the biological distinction between males and females), **gender** refers to socially learned behavior and expectations that distinguish between masculinity and femininity. Whereas biological sex identity is determined by reference to genetic and anatomical characteristics, socially learned gender is an acquired identity. We *learn*, through culturally specific socialization, how to be masculine and feminine and to assume the identities of men and women. In fact, the socialization dimension is so powerful that apparently unequivocal gender identities are formed even when biological sex is unclear (hermaphroditism) or mistaken (when the absence of a penis on a genetically male infant leads to a false identification as female).[49]

The fact of living in a "global village," thanks to new communication technologies, has helped bring gender-related issues into mainstream consciousness.[50] Because of this, women have become more aware of their inequalities everywhere in the world.[51] As Peterson and Runyan emphasize, gender equality gives birth to a more holistic way of analyzing socio-political, economic, environmental and religious structures, their interaction, and their consequences.[52]

Furthermore, as Jeanne Vickers points out, women are among the main advocates for peace in the world. "Women," she says, "have

[48] See V. Spike Peterson and Anne Sisson Runyan, *Global Gender Issues*, Boulder, San Francisco, Oxford (UK): Westview Press (Dilemmas in World Politics), 1993, p. 5.

[49] Peterson and Runyan, *Global Gender Issues*, p. 5; see also pp. 8-9; Draulans, "Human Dignity Violated by Increasing Aggression," in Haers, Hintersteiner and Schrijver (Eds.), *Postcolonial Europe in the Crucible of Cultures*, pp. 226-228.

[50] See Kate Bolick, "All the Single Ladies," in *The Atlantic*, 308/4 (2011), pp. 116-136.

[51] See Peterson and Runyan, *Global Gender Issues*, p. 12.

[52] See Peterson and Runyan, *Global Gender Issues*, p. 12.

become active in debates concerning the major questions of peace, security and international cooperation, and are involved in efforts to ensure implementations of the Nairobi Strategies [July 15-26, 1985], which provide a map for future changes to give women their rightful place in social, economic and political life."[53] This is one of the reasons why gender equality is such an important issue. "Working for a non-violent world means," says Vickers, "that women must insist upon their right to a full and fair enjoyment of human rights as set forth in the United Nations' Universal Declaration of Human Rights [December 10, 1948] and all of the covenants and conventions intended to protect and implement those rights."[54] Yet, in spite of the fact that the United Nations' Commission on the Status of Women was created in 1946, gender equality is still a big challenge, particularly for the three monotheistic religions.

In the previous chapter, I discussed the work of Leona Stucky-Abbott. She outlines very clearly how women are still diminished, in status, in Judaism and Christianity because they are not considered of the same "substance" of God as are males.[55] However, despite repeated remarks to the contrary, in fact women do not share an equal status with men in the Islamic tradition as well. Thus, gender equality remains one of the major challenges confronting the three monotheistic religions. This is not only an internal challenge to promote gender equality within these religion traditions, but also to foster gender equality in all dimensions of life, personal and social.

Riv-Ellen Prell analyzes the position of women in "Classical Reform Judaism," and the challenges women face there. She points out the importance of Jewish feminist scholars in the deconstruction of patriarchy within Judaic religion and culture. Yet, real gender equality was not envisioned as such by "Classical Reform Judaism."[56] Her conclusion is

[53] Jeanne Vickers, *Women and War*, London (UK), New Jersey: Zed Books, 1993, p. 133.

[54] Vickers *Women and War*, p. 134.

[55] See Stucky-Abbott, "The Impact of Male God Imagery on Female Identity Meaning," pp. 246, 248.

[56] See Riv-Ellen Prell, "The Vision of Woman in Classical Reform Judaism," in *Journal of the American Academy of Religion*, 50/4 (1982), p. 585. Rabbi Howard A. Berman, giving a "concise profile" of this movement, says, among other things, the following: "The term 'Classical Reform' is the most commonly used expression to denote the historic expression of Reform Judaism, as it developed in the 19th and early 20th centuries.... In essence, this tradition embodies the liberal spiritual ideas, rich intellectual foundations and broad universal vision of the early pioneers of Jewish Reform, initially in Germany, but primarily in the United States. Theologically, Classical Reform was

"that a change in gender status within a religion can never be accomplished by dismissing, minimizing, or making invisible the issue of gender."[57] These are also the conclusions drawn by Selma Koss Brandow's research on "sex equality" in Israel. In spite of the myth of sexual equality since the establishment of the State of Israel in 1948,

> this appears to have been an illusion which was more imaginary than real, and has been noted in the literature on the kibbutz where the role of women is characterized as having "regressed" and the "woman problem" is evident.... In the larger Israel society, too, the equality of women has been taken for granted but there has been little sociological investigation of their status. That research which has been done testifies to the fact that the mass of the female population exists in a subordinate "second sex" position which differs little from that of women in other parts of the world.[58]

This, as she explains, is reflected in the legal and occupational status of women and, in the dispersed women's movement which makes it much more difficult for women to make a real contribution to gender equality. Brandow concludes:

> In Israel, the myth of sexual equality continues to be perpetuated despite evidence to the contrary, while the ideology and the lip-service given to it creates strong resistance to making changes in the status quo. It is my contention that the commitment to equality which was articulated in the socialist-zionist ideology was never implemented in actuality, nor were women ever really united in search of that equality.[59]

grounded in the Biblical tradition of the Hebrew Prophets, interpreted as the emphasis on ethical action and social justice, rather than on ritual observance or ceremonial law. Intellectually, it was an outgrowth of the modern academic, scientific study of Jewish history and philosophy that emerged in Germany in the early decades of the 19th century; culturally, it reflected the transformation of Jewish communal life at that time, in response to the Emancipation of European Jewry from social isolation of the ghetto. In America, the early Reform Movement embraced the pluralistic culture of American democracy and developed a liturgy and rationale reflecting the unique experience of Judaism in the free and open society of the United States.... The Classical Reform tradition is rooted in the legacy of the 'radical' wing of the early movement, which sought a substantial revision of both synagogue worship and theological principles.... The fundamental principle of Classical Reform is that the eternal Jewish covenant with God is at the heart of our identity and history as Jews" ("Classical Reform Judaism: A Concise Profile," at http://www.renewreform.org/docs/principles.pdf [accessed September 28, 2011]).

[57] Prell, "The Vision of Woman in Classical Reform Judaism," p. 586.

[58] Selma Koss Brandow, "Ideology, Myth, and Reality: Sex Equality in Israel," in *Sex Roles*, 6/3 (1980), p. 403; see also pp. 404-419.

[59] Brandow, "Ideology, Myth, and Reality," p. 410.

Marie Andrée Roy, for her part, underlines three areas in the relationship between Catholicism and violence in which the "sacralization of males' power" is evident.[60] I consider these to indicate three of the challenges confronting the Roman Catholic Church in its efforts to foster gender equality.

The first area involves "the contempt and control of sexuality," particularly of women's sexuality and reproduction, to which I referred in the third chapter above. Contrary to this tendency, achieving gender equality will imply that women will have a right to own their sexuality. To control women's sexuality, in particular, and sexuality in general, is one of the domains where a male celibate hierarchy continues to impose limited and seemingly distorted views.

The second area to which Roy refers is "the perversion of priesthood." The Roman Catholic Church has manipulated the "common priesthood" of all baptized by focusing so much on "ordained priesthood" and making it the privilege of a particular group of celibate men. To deny women the right to be ordained priests within the Catholic tradition is seen by many as one of the major obstacles to acquiring gender equality within the Catholic Church.

Finally, the third area to which Roy points is "the relation to the truth, to obedience, and to the secret." This is, in fact, the infrastructure that sustains the rest. The Catholic hierarchy "possesses" the truth; for this reason, the faithful have to pay obedience to the teaching of the bishops and of the Pope, all of whom are surrounded by a "culture of secrecy."

In short, we have here, gathered together, all the elements for making the Roman Catholic hierarchy deeply dysfunctional and gender-biased. Achieving gender equality, on the other hand, brings us to a more relational, dynamic understanding of truth which is not the possession of anyone. Gender equality makes possible a situation in which obedience is not synonymous with the submission to patriarchal authority. Gender equality within the Church also contributes to a culture of transparency. The Roman Catholic Church will not be credible in proclaiming gender equality in the world without achieving it within its own organizational structures.

Azadeh Kian highlights how patriarchy is still present in Islam as well, serving then as a sort of counter-balance justifying resistance to

[60] See Marie Andrée Roy, "La sacralisation du pouvoir mâle," in *Relations*, 744 (2010), pp. 16-17.

efforts to arrive at gender equality. However, Islamic women's movements are also, for their part, bringing about a consciousness of the need for equality. This appears in the fact that women are challenging patriarchal structures through a better understanding of the Qur'an and Islamic traditions in order to better conciliate Islam and Modernity, "and to reclaim an egalitarian relationship between men and women."[61]

In conclusion, the three monotheistic religions carry a heavy burden on their shoulders: patriarchy. This is a burden that has not disappeared. In this regard, I fully agree with Hans Küng when he says:

> Critical questions need to be asked about the rights of women and minorities, not just in Islam. In most male-dominated world religions, the role assigned to women is problematic. For ages, women have been subjected to men, regarded as second-rate in the family, politics and the economy, and restricted in their social and religious rights and their involvement in worship. The status of women in the religions is one of the most controversial inter-cultural themes.[62]

Thus, it would be stereotyping Muslim women to believe that they are the only women discriminated against from within their own religion and culture. Violence rooted in religion and inflicted upon women crosses all cultures as well as socio-economic, political and religious structures. The same can be said for patriarchy. This is the reason why the efforts to achieve gender equality, as a global issue, are making women more aware of their dignity, rights, the sacredness of creation, and their solidarity with other women around the world in their search for justice and peace.

3. Empowered by the Healing of Shame

In the third chapter above, I indicated how, according to Redekop, unresolved "deep-rooted conflicts" contain the potential for violence.[63] Therefore, if shame, as one of the consequences of violence, can become

[61] Azadeh Kian, "Luttes feministes en islam," in *Relations*, 744 (2010), p. 18 (my translation); see also p. 19. In fact, as Hans Küng underlines, "we can understand why many Muslim women concerned with reform today are calling for a return to the Qur'an, for some legal restrictions customary for women do not in fact derive from the Qur'an, but are later juristic rulings by men. For example, there is not a word in the Qur'an about that custom which today Muslims and non-Muslims regard as typically Islamic: the wearing of the veil or headscarf by women" (*Islam*, p. 157).

[62] Küng, *Islam*, p. 562; see also pp. 563-570.

[63] See Redekop, *From Violence to Blessing*, p. 11.

a trigger for more violence, it is imperative to heal the shame inflicted upon people. When people are empowered, by freeing them from toxic, unhealthy shame, they have the potential to break the spiral of violence.

One of the most significant forms of self-alienation is that created by humiliation and arising out of shame. In order to heal wounds caused by these alienating experiences and, as a result, to become empowered as human beings and to be reconciled with ourselves, it is essential to work on transforming the sources of these powerful feelings and emotions.[64] This task of transformation is difficult because, as a society, not much attention is paid to the effects of humiliation and shame in people's lives and their functioning as triggers for violence. Thus, even if one of the sources of violence that causes humiliation and shame is physical and/or sexual abuse, "[s]hame," says Jack T. Hanford, "might have to be treated effectively before the real conscience can function and authentic ethics begin."[65]

It is often more difficult to heal wounds arising out of humiliation and shame, and indeed to get rid of the sense itself of humiliation and shame, when they are experienced as a society or as a nation. Frequently, as is the case with the occupation or domination of one country by another, these negative emotions are transmitted from one generation to the next. Thus, anger, rage, frustration, and the like cannot be overcome without eliminating the causes that give rise to them in the first place. Injustices that are inflicted fester, impacting entire future generations' prospects for peace.

The result of not treating the wound of humiliation and shame, and not coming to terms with and overcoming such humiliation and shame, at both personal and social levels, is simply more humiliation and shame and, as a consequence, more violence. Donald E. Sloat highlights this process very well: "Untreated, imposed shame eats silently away at the souls of the perpetrators and their victims, creating infections of conflict and erosion of healthy personality dynamics throughout the society, long-term consequences of which are recorded in the enormous wreckage of history."[66] To break out of the spiral of violence requires, then, that we be attentive to these powerful emotions at both personal and societal levels.

[64] See Martínez de Pisón, *Death by Despair*, pp. 74-76.

[65] Jack T. Hanford, "Destructive and Constructive Religion in Relation to Shame and Terror," in Ellens (Ed.), *The Destructive Power of Religion*, vol. 2, p. 248.

[66] Donald E. Sloat, "Imposed Shame: The Origin of Violence and Worthlessness," in Ellens (Ed.), *The Destructive Power of Religion*, vol. 3, p. 190.

In conclusion, if suffering is a common experience in our lives, there is, however, another kind of suffering that is more tragic. This is the suffering we inflict upon one another, suffering that is the result of violence in all of its forms and, in the context of our present concerns, especially violence arising out of religion. Dealing with these various forms of suffering is difficult and there is no simple answer as to how to handle them. In this regard, we have to be aware of the fact that, quite often, violence represents the "unheard voice" of humiliation and shame. To give a healthy voice to these emotions is to be empowered by the process of healing.

4. "Utopian Conception" of Globalization

In the first chapter above, I discussed the meaning of ideology, namely, the notion that what is in fact a particular truth is given an absolute, universal, value. In distinction from the notion of an ideology, we can profitably speak of a utopia, which can also refer to "unreality or a dream-world,"[67] and, thus, in a sense have a universal value. However, "[u]topia can only function as a literary story; as soon as it is taken for the reality it becomes an ideology."[68] The presence of this "dream-world," or utopia, can be found in the writings of several famous thinkers.[69] Jacques Racine refers to the positive dimension of globalization, calling it a "utopian conception." According to him, for several people,

> globalization is also the concrete expression of the desire for universal fraternity. In their observations, they see signs of the progression of this utopia; they see the development of a consciousness of being one unique humanity constituted by universal brothers and sisters according to the beautiful formula of Father de Foucauld. Does not the pursuit of globalization have the same end as catholicity? Is it not

[67] Concilium General Secretariat, "Utopia," p. 74.

[68] Concilium General Secretariat, "Utopia," p. 77; see also José María Castillo, "Utopia Set Aside," in *Concilium*, 5 (2004), pp. 38-40.

[69] See, for example, Plato, *The Republic of Plato* (A. Bloom, trans.), New York: Basic Books, 1968; Aurelius Augustinus, *The City of God against the Pagans*, (G. E. McCracken et al., trans.), Cambridge (MA): Harvard University Press, 1957–1972, 7 vols.; Thomas More (1478–1535), *Utopia: Latin Text and English Translation*, (G. M. Logan, R. M. Adams and C. H. Miller [Eds.]), Cambridge (UK): Cambridge University Press, 1995; Tommaso Campanella (1568–1639), *The City of the Sun* (D. J. Donno, trans.), Berkeley: University of California Press, 1981 and, more recently, the socialist utopia of Ernst Bloch (1885–1977), *The Principle of Hope* (N. Plaice, S. Plaice and P. Knight, trans.), Cambridge (MA): MIT Press (Studies in Contemporary German Social Thought), 1986, 3 vols.

> opposed to the entrenchments in one's own identity which have generated so much violence in the past and in the present? Is not this phenomenon one step toward the achievement of the vow formulated by Christ: "[T]hat they may all be one"? [Jn 17:21] Is it not a veritable sign of the times, according to the theology of Vatican II?[70]

Here, globalization as utopia can be considered as the process through which new socio-political, financial and monetary systems,[71] along with a new environmental order contribute to justice and equality. To overcome alienation, humiliation and shame within people and between nations, we need to take an active role in working toward greater justice and equality at so many different social levels.[72]

Additionally, it is necessary to take into account the role that religions can play in this positively viewed process of globalization. As Jacques Haers notes, "religions, churches and religious organizations constitute important global and international networks, profoundly influencing the minds and deep convictions of millions of people."[73] Their contribution to peace is not limited to interreligious dialogue but also to denouncing "global social iniquity,"[74] as we will see in the next chapter.

5. Remembering and Truth

In order to heal the wounds and eliminate the consequences of violence, in its personal and social dimensions, people have to enter into a process of remembering and truth.[75] Remembering the events that caused humiliation and shame, in order to discern the truth of what happened, is the only way of moving from evil to goodness, from lies to truth, and from violence to peace. Remembering, therefore, helps individuals and communities identify and cope with the truth of the circumstances surrounding their respective traumas.

[70] Racine, "Les formes de violence émergeant de la mondialisation," in Noël (Ed.), *Mondialisation, violence et religion*, pp. 32-33 (my translation).

[71] See Pontifical Council for Justice and Peace, "Toward Reforming the International Financial and Monetary Systems in the Context of Global Public Authority [October 24, 2011]," in *Origins*, 41/22 (2011), pp. 341-349.

[72] See Omar, "Overcoming Religiously Motivated Violence," pp. 81-82.

[73] Haers, "Introduction," in Haers, Hintersteiner and Schrijver (Eds.), *Postcolonial Europe in the Crucible of Cultures*, p. 5.

[74] Hanson, *Religion and Politics in the International System Today*, p. 61.

[75] See Ramón Martínez de Pisón, "Enrichie par la guérison," in *Counseling et Spiritualité*, 30/1 (2011), pp. 16-19.

Memory plays an essential role in the process of forgiveness and reconciliation involving individuals, groups and institutions. As Jan Assmann emphasizes, "[t]he only solution [to helping people to forget] is to acknowledge other people's memories and to negotiate a common past in which the suffering of the other side and one's own share of the guilt have their proper place."[76] The healing of memories is rooted precisely in the capacity to remember;[77] this is why memory is so essential in psychoanalysis. To push people who have been abused and traumatized to forget is "nonsensical." Lee Griffith explains:

> The denial of remembered traumas and the loss of the ability to integrate these memories is what psychologists call "dissociation." While dissociation may be an understandable reaction to trauma, it is not the path of healing. Whether the trauma is childhood abuse or the devastation of war, recovery requires remembrance and mourning. The advice to "forgive and forget" is nonsensical. Forgiveness requires memory.[78]

Remembering is not synonymous with further victimization of the self.[79] To victimize oneself means that a person surrenders his or her power to others. Often individuals consider their parents, society, and religious institutions responsible for their problems. However, not only

[76] Jan Assmann, *Religion and Cultural Memory: Ten Studies*, Stanford: Stanford University Press (Cultural Memory in the Present), 2006, p. 21; see also J. Shawn Landres and Oren Baruch Stier, "Introduction," in Oren Baruch Stier and J. Shawn Landres (Eds.), *Religion, Violence, Memory, and Place*, Bloomington: Indiana University Press, 2006, pp. 1-12.

[77] Marc Gopin, speaking on the conflict between Arabs and Jews in the Middle East, says: "It would be powerful indeed if groups of Arabs and Jews, perhaps aided by sympathetic Western Christians–who also have a key role in causing and healing this tragic conflict–would begin, *in detail*, to mourn what was lost. They must begin to visit the dead together, to bury them together in symbolic ways, to memorialize lost lives and lost homes. They need to talk about the losses for as long as it is necessary, to thoroughly indulge the past rather than suppress it, to let go of the fear that it would disrupt rational dialogue and conversation. We must do exactly what rational peacemakers have tried to suppress, namely, we must indulge memory. But we must do it, not destructively as it is indulged in the privacy of particular groups, but as a part of peacemaking, as part of an effort to honor each group's memories at the same time that we struggle constructively over the present.

"One cannot really escape the morass of deadly conflict and discover life again after death without this kind of healing of memory" (*Between Eden and Armageddon*, pp. 173-174; see also p. 190).

[78] Griffith, *The War on Terrorism and the Terror of God*, p. 38; see also Brudholm and Cushman, "Introduction," in Brudholm and Cushman (Eds.), *The Religious in Responses to Mass Atrocity*, pp. 1-2.

[79] See Martínez de Pisón, "Enrichie par la guérison," pp. 21-23.

is this disempowering, but it also renders them dependent on others. Remembering helps one regain one's power and ensures that abuse will not be repeated. Regrettably, there is a tendency to try to forget traumatic events.[80] Institutions are not so much interested in forgiving as they are in forgetting. They try to erase the memory of what they do not wish to be remembered.

This unhealthy and ideological tendency is present in socio-political institutions as well as in religious ones. For example, as was highlighted in the third chapter above, there has been an all too widespread inclination to silence any reference to, or even to hide, physical, sexual, and cultural abuses inflicted upon children and adolescents by the clergy and members of the hierarchy of different churches. If religious authorities have finally begun to remember such abuses, if they have started to speak the truth about what happened, it is because they have been obliged, even forced, to do it.[81] Such inclination to silence rather than to remember shows itself, for example, at socio-political levels when minorities continue to be exploited by more powerful majorities. The practice of silencing victims' voices is even more tragic when it is done in God's name, whether in religious traditions or on a more socio-political level. Surely, in any of these circumstances, people are using God's name wrongfully.

To take an extreme example, this terrible experience of silencing happened in Nazi concentration camps in occupied Europe:

> The Nazis accompanied their violence and killing with various efforts to silence the voices of their victims, to shatter their frameworks of meaning, and to make thought of any depth impossible.... Survivors of atrocity sometimes suffer from an inability to speak–they may begin choking or stuttering, break down in tears, fall silent while trying to explain what happened, in some cases unable to begin to speak again–because of the violence inflicted on them that sought to discredit, silence, and finally erase their voices.
>
> The sense of impossibility was further compounded by the limited capacities of listeners to understand or imagine such extreme events.[82]

[80] See Geddes, "Religious Rhetoric in Response to Atrocity," in Brudholm and Cushman (Eds.), *The Religious in Responses to Mass Atrocity*, pp. 23-24.

[81] See Richard G. Malloy, "[Pedophilia/Sexual Abuse] From 'Sin' and 'Compulsion' to 'Crime': Trying to Understand the Crisis of the Past 25 Years," in *The Priest*, 67/2 (February, 2011), pp. 10-13, 24; Christopher Lamb and Sam Adams, "Putting a Price on Damaged Lives," in *The Tablet*, January 29, 2011, pp. 4-5.

[82] Geddes, "Religious Rhetoric in Response to Atrocity," in Brudholm and Cushman (Eds.), *The Religious in Responses to Mass Atrocity*, pp. 23-24; see also E. B. Anderson, "Memory, Tradition, and the Re-Membering of Suffering," in *Religious Education*, 105/2 (2010), pp. 124-139.

In the third chapter above, I referred to the importance of paying attention to the victims of violence, namely, to listening to their voices. This is not an easy task, but it is essential for overcoming the negative, and oftentimes lethal, consequences of violence. As Geddes notes, many survivors of atrocities have lost the capacity to name their suffering and to put words to it. Victims, then, can suffer further due to their difficulty in expressing what they have gone through and, consequently, in finding an empathic listener. Yet, as Chris Hedges points out, "[u]ntil there is a common vocabulary and a shared historical memory there is no peace in any society, only an absence of war."[83]

In this sense, North American culture has privatized suffering in all its dimensions. As such, it can become very uncomfortable for us to listen to someone else speaks of his or her physical pain or psychological suffering. This tendency is wonderfully described by Henri J. M. Nouwen (1932–1996) in his keynote address on compassion to the Annual Convention of the Catholic Health Association of Canada (Ottawa, May 15, 1979). In it, he refers to the fact that to be compassionate means to join the other person in his or her pain and suffering. To be compassionate means to be with the pain and suffering of the other person, to listen to him or her, and not to give quick solutions:

> You feel a nervous tension inside and you begin to wonder what you can possible say when he stops talking! We feel uncomfortable around people in [physical] pain [and/or suffering] and we want to do anything and everything to get away from it. So, to feel compassionate is not always an immediate and natural response. In many ways, it is a very difficult way of living.[84]

For these reasons, within the three monotheistic traditions, religious communities and their leaders and members need to develop a pastoral approach to listening, grounded in compassion. When confronted by other people's pain and suffering, religious leaders and communities should listen instead of moralizing or giving justification for the suffering experienced by innocent victims.

[83] Hedges, *War is a Force That Gives Us Meaning*, p. 81; see also pp. 141, 176.

[84] Henri J. M. Nouwen, "Reflections on Compassion," in *Catholic Health Association of Canada Review*, 8/4 (1980), p. 5; see also pp. 4, 6-9.

6. Paradigm of Peace

In the introduction to the first chapter above, I indicated that peace, justice, solidarity, love, mercy, compassion and forgiveness belong to the very heart of the three monotheistic religions. Alas, as I have discussed, these traditions have themselves contributed to the justification of violence in numerous ways. To counteract this perversion of religion, it is vital to explore the capacities of these religions to build peace.

As I have mentioned at the end of the Introduction to this book, peace consists not only in the absence of war and violence: it consists also in the expression of a life lived in solidarity with others, with creation and with God. Peace is, then, intrinsically linked to righteousness and justice. I believe that peace is the most important criterion for discerning the "authenticity" of a religion and the "veracity" of its Holy Scripture.

Peace should also be, as Nelson-Pallmeyer points out, the source of a dialogue among all religious denominations: "The search for alternatives to violence in a wounded world could well be the common bond that brings together Jews, Christians, Muslims, and many other people of diverse faiths to create a world that better reflects the compassion many believers attribute to God."[85] In a world characterized by growing religiously motivated violence, peace should be the goal of interreligious dialogue. As Clinton Bennett indicates, "[a]n alternative, peace affirming understanding of religion is needed if religion is to survive."[86] Thus, peace is not only the "soul" of religion but also its "lungs".

If the more immediate goal of interreligious dialogue can be reformulated as a common search for peace, the second contribution that Judaism, Christianity, and Islam can make to an itinerary of peace is tolerance. As R. Scott Appleby states, "[t]o be tolerant, then, is to resist the temptation to use violence, or forcible action, against an individual or group of which one disapproves. Tolerance... [is] an attitude bespeaking respect for and defense of the rights of others."[87] As was mentioned in the previous chapter, Richard G. Cote and J. Harold Ellens recall

[85] Nelson-Pallmeyer, *Is Religion Killing Us?*, p. 108; see also Mooren, *War and Peace in Monotheistic Religions*, pp. 153-154, 186-197.

[86] Clinton Bennett, *In Search of Solutions: The Problem of Religion and Conflict*, London (UK) and Oakville: Equinox Publishing Ltd. (Religion and Violence), 2008, p. 8.

[87] R. Scott Appleby, *The Ambivalence of the Sacred: Religion, Violence, and Reconciliation*, Lanham: Rowman & Littlefield Publishers, Inc. (Carnegie Commission on Preventing Deadly Conflict Series), 2000, p. 14.

that intolerance of ambiguity is one of the characteristics of religious fundamentalism. To learn to live with ambiguity, an essential dimension of human life, is also a *conditio sine qua non* for building peace:

> From a religious point of view, then, living with ambiguity is the consequence of the distance between the infinite God and the contingent human being.... Ambiguity characterizes human experience, as any adult well knows, because reality presents itself as a series of interacting changes with often unpredictable effects, leading one to choose among variously imperfect courses and competing explanations and forcing one to accept the consequences of the decision.[88]

To be tolerant does not mean losing particular cultural and religious identities and values, nor giving up one's principles, nor agreeing necessarily with someone else's way of living. To be tolerant means to respect others' diversity at a personal as well as at institutional and social levels.

In addition to working through interreligious dialogue for peace and tolerance, believers within the three monotheistic religions should engage in peacemaking processes, particularly becoming true pacifists. As Stassen and Gushee note, "[p]acifism comes from the Latin, *pax facere*, to make peace."[89] In order to become a peacemaker, one needs to move from demonizing others to seeing them through God's eyes. "For religious peacemakers," says Sharon Erickson Nepstad, "the line between good and evil lies within each individual, not between groups."[90] This also means that no one is lost forever and, contrary to the way in which some terrorists define religion, namely, as "*an end in itself*," for peacemakers, religion is "*a means to an end*, namely, enlightenment, truth, or spiritual fulfillment.... Moreover, many religious peacemakers hold that the type of vessel one uses to reach the shore is not so important."[91] Together with working for peace, religions have a role to play in the search for justice, as I will propose in the next chapter.[92]

[88] Appleby, *The Ambivalence of the Sacred*, p. 29; see also p. 30.

[89] Stassen and Gushee, *Kingdom Ethics*, p. 167.

[90] Nepstad, "Religion, Violence, and Peacemaking," p. 298. Willard M. Swartly points out the importance of Jesus' Beatitudes (Mt 5–7) in the peacemaking process for Christians, and for every man and woman of good will (see *Covenant of Peace*, pp. 56-57, 190).

[91] Nepstad, "Religion, Violence, and Peacemaking," p. 300. On the next page, Nepstad adds: "For religious peacemakers, therefore, the goal is spiritual enlightenment and truth–not only for individuals but also for society as a whole. This is not to be confused with religious terrorists' desire to establish a religious government or culture but rather to integrate religiously inspired principles of justice and respect for all people into the fabric of society."

[92] See Swartly, *Covenant of Peace*, p. 143.

Finally, religious and spiritual leaders of the three monotheistic religions should deal together with the toxic texts of their Holy Scriptures.[93] They must educate believers to the peace that lies at the heart of their religious traditions and encourage them to become peacemakers. Thus, "[w]e must reformulate our traditions' theological understandings of men, women, marriage, suffering, and obedience so that they cannot be used as tools against those who struggle to find freedom from violence."[94]

I would like to conclude this part by reminding readers of what Hans Küng has repeatedly stressed in several of his publications regarding the future of religions:

> In contrast to antiquity and the Middle Ages, in the twenty-first century humankind can destroy itself with novel technical means. Therefore all religions, including the three prophetic religions which are often so aggressive, should be concerned to avoid wars and promote peace. A careful re-reading of one's own religious traditions is unavoidable.[95]

Then, he brings to a close the last book of his trilogy on the three monotheistic religions with the following words:

> No peace among the nations
> without peace among the religions.
>
> No peace among the religions
> without dialogue between the religions.
>
> No dialogue between the religions
> without global ethical standards.
>
> No survival of our globe without
> a global ethic, a world ethic,
> supported by both
> the religious and the non-religious.[96]

Living according to a paradigm of peace, including fostering justice and solidarity, is not an option or a kind of decoration for religions, particularly for Judaism, Christianity, and Islam. It is a moral obligation. To be peacemakers is the only way to foster a culture of peace. How can we live in a culture of peace if people see religions justifying, or at least religions being used to justify, the most terrible acts of violence? To educate

93 See Omar, "Overcoming Religiously Motivated Violence," p. 79.
94 Nienhuis, "Theological Reflections on Violence and Abuse," p. 123.
95 Küng, *Islam*, p. 602.
96 Küng, *Islam*, pp. 661-662.

believers, and people in general, to be engaged in the transformation of violence into peace, justice, love, mercy, compassion and solidarity is the best way of giving testimony to the God of our ancestors, Abraham, Isaac, Jacob. This is the same God in whom Jews, Christians, and Muslims believe. Peace, then, should be at the center of a global religious ecumenism and, beyond any doctrinal religious differences, is what should unite believers in the common endeavor of a better world.

Two important recent interreligious events have had as their purpose the launching of such an urgent call to peace. The first of these events was the Second Global Conference on World's Religions after September 11, which had as its theme "Peace through Religion." The Conference was organized by McGill University in cooperation with the Université de Montréal and was held at the Montréal Palais des congrès on September 7, 2011. The Conference brought together persons playing an important role in the area of the world's religions. Among these persons were the following: His Holiness, the Fourteenth Dalai Lama; Deepak Chopra, a world renowned author and physician; Robert A. Thurman, Professor in Indo-Tibetan Studies at Columbia University; Tariq Ramadan, Professor of Contemporary Islamic Studies at Oxford University; Gregory Baum, Professor in the Faculty of Religious Studies at McGill University; and Steven T. Katz, Director of the Elie Wiesel Centre for Judaic Studies and Professor of Religion at Boston University. Conference participants formulated and approved three Resolutions,[97] the last of which dealt with revising the Universal Declaration of Human Rights, a Declaration previously made on December 10, 1998, by the Conference on the World's Religions. Article 18, section 3, of this Declaration reads: "Everyone has the duty to promote peace and tolerance among different religions and ideologies."[98]

The gathering in Montréal coincided with the tenth anniversary of September 11, 2001. In taking a look at the celebrations commemorating this anniversary, we can see verified what I have been saying throughout the present study. First, we can note the lasting consequences of violence perpetrated upon innocent people and the difficulty we have in grieving on the occasion of the death of loved ones.[99] Second, we sense

[97] The three Resolutions, together with all the documentation regarding this conference, can be found at http://www.gcwr2011.org (accessed October 25, 2011)

[98] Text cited from http://www.gcwr2011.org/pdf/UDHRWR_en.pdf (accessed October 25, 2011).

[99] See Chris Matthew Sciabarra, "Ten Years Later," at http://www.nyu.edu/projects/sciabarra/essays/wtcremember11.htm (accessed November 19, 2011).

the persistent feelings of humiliation and shame experienced by Americans, humiliation and shame that, as I have already mentioned, risk becoming a source of further violence.[100] Third, we recognize continuing biases against Muslim people taken as a whole.[101] Finally, we see the perduring political and religious use of this tragedy of September 11, 2001, verified once more in the belief by Americans that "God is with us." This belief finds concrete expression in President Barack H. Obama's reading from Psalm 46:11 at the commemorative ceremony in New York City on September 11, 2011.[102] Given all this, we see why the world's religions have the obligation to foster healing and reconciliation if we wish to live in peace.

The second of these events was the "Day of Reflection, Dialogue and Prayer for Peace and Justice in the World," which took place in the Italian town of Assisi on October 27, 2011. Pope Benedict XVI sponsored this "Day" in order to mark the twenty-fifth anniversary of the first interreligious day of prayer for peace held at the request of the late Pope John Paul II (1920-2005) in the same city on October 27, 1986. The theme of this second encounter was "Pilgrims of Truth, Pilgrims of Peace," and was attended by "some 300 religious leaders from around the world–including Christians, Jews, Muslims, Hindus, Zoroastrians, Taoists, Shintoists and Buddhists,"[103] in addition to Agnostics and Atheists. During this second gathering, participants placed great emphasis on the fact that there is a direct relationship among truth, justice and peace. For peace is not something that can be imposed by force. Rather, it emerges through the recognition and respect of legitimate differences among peoples and religions. Peace is the result of a common endeavor

[100] See Clark McCauley, "The Psychology of U.S. Reaction to 9/11," at http://www.psychologytoday.com/blog/friction/201109/the-psychology-us-reaction-911 (accessed November 19, 2011); Alan Mozes, "9/11 Left Permanent Scars on the American Psyche," at http://www.erietvnews.com/story/15435046/911-left-permanent-scars-on-the-american-psyche (accessed November 19, 2011).

[101] See Matt Apuzzo and Adam Goldman (Associated Press), "Name Changes Seen as Red Flag by NYPD [New York Police Department], Records Show," at http://www.freep.com/article/20111027/NEWS07/110270665/Name-changes-seen-red-flag-by-NYPD-records-show (accessed November 19, 2011).

[102] See "Remarks by the President at the September 11th 10th Anniversary Commemoration," at http://historymusings.wordpress.com/2011/09/11/full-text-september-11-2011-president-barack-obama-remarks-911-10th-anniversary-memorial-nyc-reading-psalm-46 (accessed November 19, 2011).

[103] Philip Pullella, "Pope Expresses Shame for Christian Violence in History," at http://in.reuters.com/article/2011/10/27/idINIndia-60153620111027 (accessed October 27, 2011).

carried out by all, and especially by believers and religious leaders, to promote justice and solidarity in the world. This road to peace becomes the royal way to overcome fundamentalist attitudes which deform the truth and give rise to division, discrimination and violence.[104]

* * *

Moving from violence to peace, a peace characterized by righteousness, justice, solidarity, love, mercy and compassion, is one of the most important, if difficult, tasks of every religious tradition. If violence, in all its manifestations, engenders so much suffering, humiliation, shame and death, it is even more perverse when it is done in God's name. In this case, religion loses its capacity to bring people into true contact with the Divine. It becomes an ideology and its worship is transformed into idolatry. For these reasons, the fifth conclusion that can be drawn from our study is that religion must be considered as incompatible with violence.

To cultivate this understanding, believers and religious leaders need to recover what is at the core of their religious traditions. For the three monotheistic religions, this means recovering and reemphasizing the basic notion and importance of the love of God for humanity and creation, God's universal Covenant with all people. By recovering this core belief, the three monotheistic religions will continue to have an important, and positive, role to play in public life. I will speak more of this role in the next chapter.

[104] See Pope Benedict XVI, "Assisi 2011: Pilgrims of Truth, Pilgrims of Peace," in *Origins*, 41/23 (2011), pp. 357-360; Rowan Williams, "Assisi 2011: We Are Not Strangers to Each Other," in *Origins*, 41/23 (2011), pp. 360-361; Olav Fykse Tveit, "Assisi 2011: Re-establishing Peace for Jerusalem," in *Origins*, 41/23 (2011), pp. 361-362; David Rosen, "Assisi 2011: Peace Is the Name of God," in *Origins*, 41/23 (2011), pp. 362-363; Kyai Haji Hasyim Muzadi, "Assisi 2011: Religion Misused for Nonreligious Purposes," in *Origins*, 41/23 (2011), pp. 363-364; Julia Kristeva, "Assisi 2011: What Is Humanism?," in *Origins*, 41/23 (2011), pp. 364-365.

Chapter 6

Religion and Public Life

Transcendence as such, or the openness of human beings to a reality truly beyond themselves, has not disappeared from Western society, and this even in the face of a culture that has often tried to silence any expression of such openness which is, in the end, so deeply rooted in what we are as persons. Faith, as an expression of this openness, then, is an essential dimension of any person who lives in the world and is open to a larger frame of reference, that is, of meaning.[1] Thus, it is important to nourish this essential dimension of human life.[2]

In spite of critiques by the "masters of suspicion,"[3] religion has not disappeared from societies and cultures around the world. Interest in religion and spirituality remains widespread, even though the search for transcendence has become more dispersed, so to speak, and with less of a distinct focus on a specific reality beyond the everyday.[4] Psychologists and medical doctors are presently introducing into their practice and research the notion and value of the role that religion plays in life and healing.[5] In

[1] See M. Kathryn Armistead, *God-Images in the Healing Process*, Minneapolis: Fortress Press, 1995, pp. xvi, 86; James W. Jones, *In the Middle of this Road We Call Our Life: The Courage to Search for Something More*, San Francisco: HarperSanFrancisco (Psychology/Spirituality), 1995, pp. 3, 187; James W. Fowler, *Stages of Faith: The Psychology of Human Development and the Quest for Meaning*, New York: Harper & Row, 1981, p. 4.

[2] See Jones, *In the Middle of this Road We Call Our Life*, pp. 119-120; Fowler, *Stages of Faith*, pp. 1-36.

[3] Paul Ricoeur (1913–2005)'s way of referring to Ludwig A. Feuerbach (1804–1872), Karl Marx (1818–1883), Friedrich W. Nietzsche (1844–1900) and Sigmund Freud (1856–1939). See André Comte-Sponsoville, "Les prophètes de la mort de Dieu," in *Le Monde des Religions*, 49 (2011), pp. 22-25.

[4] See Lucy Bregman, *Beyond Silence and Denial: Death and Dying Reconsidered*, Louisville: Westminster John Knox Press, 1999, p. 7; Lucy Bregman, *Death and Dying, Spirituality and Religions: A Study of the Death Awareness Movement*, New York: Peter Lang Publishing, Inc. (American University Studies. Series VII: Theology and Religion, 228), 2003, pp. 33-35; David B. Perrin, *Studying Christian Spirituality*, New York, London (UK): Routledge (Religion and Spirituality), 2007.

[5] See Joan Connell, "Medical Schools Realize that Doctors Must Understand Religious Faith," in *Prairie Messenger*, 73/18 (1995), p. 20; Ioma Hawkins and Silvia L. Bullock, "Informed Consent and Religious Values: A Neglected Area of Diversity," in *Psychotherapy*, 32/2 (1995), pp. 293-294; Joseph K. Neuman and Frederick Leppien, "Impact of Religious Values and Medical Specialty on Professional Inservice Decisions," in *Journal*

psychology, for example, one does not tend anymore to link an interest in religious phenomena with an underdeveloped stage in human life. In short, religion is no longer considered an illusion, or the projection of an alienated conscience, as Feuerbach and Marx thought, nor a neurosis, as Freud affirmed. Rather, religion and a possible religious commitment have come to be seen as an essential dimension of the person[6] that is rooted in the dynamic of human development itself.[7] The perduring openness to some form of transcendent reality, faith seen as a constitutive dimension of the human person, and the more recently developed appreciation, in psychology and medicine, to the importance of one's religious commitment, help explain why religion is still widely present in today's world, and why it can and should become a powerful player and partner in the process of moving from violence to peace.[8]

In the first part of this chapter, I will explore what I call "the taboo of privacy." At least in the West, privacy, in its negative connotation, refers to secrecy, to what should remain hidden. This way of perceiving privacy has negatively affected religion, defining it then as a private matter. In the second part of this chapter, I will examine the negative effects of considering religion as private. Considering religion as a purely private matter is contrary to its most important dimension, namely, the fact that religion is rooted in the very heart of the human person. If the person is open to the other, to creation, and to God, and if religion is rooted in the heart of the person, then, as I will stress in the third part of this chapter, religion has an important role to play in the search for cultural identity and in the transformation of the socio-political, economic and environmental structures that contribute to peace, justice and solidarity.[9]

of Psychology and Theology, 25/4 (1997), pp. 437, 445; Bregman, *Death and Dying, Spirituality and Religions*, pp. 13-31.

[6] See Ana María Rizzuto, *The Birth of the Living God: A Psychoanalytic Study*, Chicago: The University of Chicago Press, 1979, p. 47.

[7] See Jones, *In the Middle of this Road We Call Our Life*, p. 15.

[8] Francisco Díez de Velasco is one of those who advocates for religion's role in today's world as "a resource used in settings where the main causes of events are of a geostrategic, economic, or political nature. Therefore, the solution to violence cannot be simply to eliminate or de-socialize religion. A formula within our reach is that of cohabiting with difference: learning to live in a progressively multireligious and multicultural world respecting the richness of diversity, while at the same time seeking some minimally consensual points of view which will allow for a life in common without having to resort to violence" ("Theoretical Reflections on Violence and Religion," pp. 114-115).

[9] The relationship between religion and public life has also become a topic of interest from an academic point of view. In this regard, Carleton University (Ottawa, Canada), as of the Fall of 2011, offers a Master of Arts Program in Religion and Public Life (see http://www.carleton.ca/chum/religionpubliclife [accessed November 3, 2011]).

1. Privacy as a Form of Taboo in Western Society

In the fourth chapter above, I referred to the importance of so-called healthy shame and its positive role in human life. Healthy shame is a way in and through which the self protects itself and its identity against invasive intruders. It sets boundaries that others cannot, or at least should not, trespass. In an analogous sense, privacy also carries with it a positive connotation as well. Like healthy shame, privacy can protect an individual from the unwanted, even inappropriate, scrutiny of others. Richard G. Cote presents what could be considered the core of American cultural values enjoining one to be "FREE, STRONG, ENTERPRISING, and INNOVATIVE."[10] I would add "private" to this list.

As it was with toxic, negative, unhealthy shame, in some ways what is identified as private has become taboo, something that is not spoken of and which should not be communicated to others. Privacy has been made into an idol, so to speak and has become the prevailing attitude we are to take especially in certain areas more directly touching and related to affectivity. Though in today's society much of the taboo related to sexuality has been removed, there has arisen a real taboo of privacy, so to speak, and of the affective life.[11] This stress on the notion of privacy can, as I mentioned in the previous chapter, lead many victims to lose the capacity to speak of their physical pain and/or psychological suffering. They fear being exposed, and often the pain and suffering of these victims are considered inappropriate topics to be brought up in public discourse. Such topics are, then, often relegated to the sphere of the "private."

It is important to situate the connection between religion and privacy within the larger influence that individualism, as distinct from individuality, is having in Western societies, particularly in North America. Individualism, and here more specifically religious individualism, can be considered a reaction to an overly institutionalized religion that does not allow the person to develop a genuinely personalized way of experiencing transcendence.

A healthier and less extreme sense of privacy is very different from what I have called "savage subjectivism,"[12] or the tendency to consider

[10] Richard G. Cote, *Re-Visioning Mission: The Catholic Church and Culture in Postmodern America*, New York, Mahwah: Paulist Press, 1996, p. 135.

[11] See Ramón Martínez de Pisón, "Savoir apprivoiser la mort: Angoisse et plénitude de vie," in *Counseling et Spiritualité*, 27/1 (2008), pp. 89-105.

[12] See Ramón Martínez de Pisón, "La dialectique de la foi aujourd'hui: Entre la subjetivité 'sauvage' et le traditionalism 'intégriste'," in *Église et Théologie*, 25/3 (1994), pp. 405-423.

oneself as the only point of reference for everything outside a person's own individual universe and personal beliefs. Likewise, such a more positive sense of privacy is different from that in which one is closed to others in the sense of being unable to share with them one's feelings and beliefs. It differs as well from an attitude according to which one is concerned only with one's own life in an individualistic way. Privacy, like modesty, is not necessarily opposed to otherness. On the contrary, rightly understood, privacy is the respect for one's own intimacy and a reasonable effort to protect that intimacy from being invaded by others, oftentimes due to their morbid curiosity.[13] Yet, the idolization of privacy has negatively affected religion, its practice and its various legitimate roles.

2. Confusing Private and Personal

Religion involves what is most personal and intimate in the life of a person, namely, that person's openness to the transcendent and the beyond. The practice of religion is in fact the exercise of giving expression to this most important dimension of the human person. However, here personal and intimate are not to be considered synonymous with what is private or hidden from others. Religion is not a hidden element of peoples' lives. Rather, by its very nature religion implies alterity, the opening of the person to others, to creation, and to God, all of which are then constitutive elements of religion as such.

More widely stated, a healthy sense of privacy does not keep human beings from setting up a network of relationships. Indeed, people discover their gifts, their talents, and who they are through the eyes of those who recognize and receive them, particularly through the eyes of those who love them.[14] Only in the presence of another human being can one discover oneself as human.

[13] See Martínez de Pisón, *Death by Despair*, pp. 76-78. However, we are experiencing a contradiction in our way of living. In a sense, we have become extremely jealous of our own privacy, which we tend to protect to the extreme. In another sense, we have developed a kind of morbid curiosity regarding the private lives of important persons, about which we would like to know the most mundane details. We scrutinize the private lives of artists, politicians, and public figures with a magnifying glass. Perhaps to fill up the emptiness in our own lives.

[14] See See Henri J. M. Nouwen, *Reaching Out: The Three Movements of the Spiritual Life*, Garden City: Doubleday & Company Inc., 1975, p. 61; Sue Chance, *Stronger than Death*, New York, London (UK): W. W. Norton & Company, 1992, p. 101; Martínez de Pisón, *God*, pp. 20-21. Donald Capps says the following regarding the importance of

In a more religious reference, the book of Genesis expresses this correctly. I am intrinsically related to the other as one who reveals to me my own humanity. We can immediately note that becoming conscious of the ontological equality between man and woman comes about, as expressed in the Yahwist tradition (Gn 2:20-23), through such an encounter. Adam recognizes himself as a human being only in the face of another human being, Eve. Furthermore, their mutual dependence is expressed by their nudity (Gn 2:25) that does not have any merely sexual connotation here. Rather, their nudity is the expression of their more general relatedness, of their being situated in relation to each other. Nudity also represents the constitutive fragility of the human being, a being that does not have in him or herself the foundation of his or her life, but who receives life as a gift. Accepting oneself as naked here means to overcome any possessive and dominating tendencies. It is only when Adam and Eve did not accept themselves as naked beings, that is, finding the ultimate meaning of their lives in their relationship with the divine Other, that nakedness became synonymous with shame (Gn 3:7-10).

Therefore, as I indicated in the first chapter above, we can see again that others are not enemies, but people who reflect one's own self. This mirroring from others is essential for human development. It permits others to share their innermost feelings and emotions with us and we with them. Contrary to an old interpretation which defined the person as "the consciousness of oneself in opposition to another," namely, the affirmation that "I am I because I am not you," a person is a being "with." This "with" belongs to our very nature as person. A person is then connected to reality, to others, to creation, and to the transcendent. The human person is a being "open to." To discover the other as other, and not as the projection of my own needs, is the fulfillment of human development.

Religion is, then, a constitutive dimension of the person and not a private affair.[15] To try to reduce religion to the sphere of privacy in the

the other for discovering one's own self: "Our real self is discovered through the recognition that we receive from one another, in the moment that our self-affirmation is affirmed by the other. The source of self-knowing is not private introspection but the mutual mirroring of selves" (*The Depleted Self: Sin in a Narcissistic Age*, Minneapolis: Fortress Press, 1993, p. 166).

[15] See Ramón Martínez de Pisón, "Quand je dis 'je crois en Dieu', qui est ce 'je' qui exprime sa foi?: De l'"être réel' à l'"être possible' chez Maurice Zundel," in *Counseling et Spiritualité*, 29/1 (2010), pp. 40-42.

name of a secular State, as if secularity were synonymous with religious neutrality, is to fall into a laicistic ideology. This ideology suggests that there is a completely neutral, secular, State. Yet the person is a public being. Thus, if religion is personal, and if the person is a public being, religion also has a public dimension. Accordingly, people have the right to publically confess their religion and to have their rights recognized in this regard. What is important, then, is not the proclamation of the religious neutrality of the State as such, which is often the manifestation of a "reverse discrimination" against particular religious denominations that were powerful in the past but, rather, of the State being at the service of all its people, believers or not. For this reason, the State should endeavor to make "reasonable accommodations" to the different religious communities participating in public life.[16]

If religion is to be considered authentic, it must as both personal and social engage people in the transformation of injustice at all levels of society. An authentic religion should, therefore, encourage its faithful to become engaged in public life. In this regard, Benoît Bégin states:

> Human existence is fundamentally political and social; one becomes human through a culture, language, within a community, and a society. Dialogue and exchange are fundamental to humanity. Under these conditions, spirituality [and religion] cannot have their origin in solitary reflection, enclosed within its own points of view and its own individual positions. Personal and spiritual growth cannot occur independently of the requirements of our relationship with others.[17]

To encourage the engagement of religious believers in public life, we need to rediscover and reemphasize the cultural and socio-political dimensions of religion. Besides religion's overall potential contribution to peace, the fact that religion has these cultural and socio-political dimensions means that religion can and should play an essential role in more focused searches for meaning, justice, forgiveness, and reconciliation.

[16] See Charles Taylor, "Religion Is Not the Problem: Secularism & Democracy," in *Commonweal*, CXXXVIII/4 (2011), pp. 17-21.

[17] Benoît Bégin, "Croissance spirituelle et engagement social: Une complémentarité," in Marc Dumas et François Nault (Eds.), *Pluralisme religieux et quêtes spirituelles: Incidences théologiques*, Montréal, Fides (Héritage et Projet, 67), 2004, pp. 86-87 (my translation); see also François Bousquet, "Pour une Église qui fasse signe en Europe," in *Esprit & Vie*, 211 (2009), p. 42.

3. Cultural and Socio-Political Dimensions of Religion

"To give religion its due respect is the beginning of wisdom."[18] This expression contradicts the now commonplace Western distinction between private and public regarding religion, a distinction rooted in the eighteenth century European Enlightenment[19] and in effect announces that such a distinction can no longer serve as an adequate paradigm for understanding religion in contemporary life.

In relationship to the role of religion as an instrument of social harmony and cultural identity, as highlighted in the first chapter above, James K. Wellman, Jr., points out that "[r]eligion[,] like politics, forms identities and thus the two cannot help but move in relation to one another, sometimes antagonistically and sometimes in tandem."[20] Religion provides a larger horizon of meaning in human life, thereby contributing to the sense that life is not reduced to pure immanence. Human beings need not only to live but also to have reasons to live. They need to understand. It is because of these needs that people integrate new events and experiences within a larger frame of reference. Religion can also open a person's frame of reference from the inside out. This is why religion can be considered as inserted into the core of human life itself. The religious dimension of human experience opens the person to his or her inmost being. Religion, then, is a contributor to identify formation and meaning. In this regard, as Eric O. Hanson writes, "[t]aking religion seriously offers a much broader spectrum of political possibilities."[21]

Therefore, even though religion can, as we have stressed, be a source of violence and a factor in bringing it about, it can and should also be an important resource in confronting it. This is why there is a need to consider religion, as Philip L. Tite states, as a partner in the reflection on terrorism: "However, one of the most obvious factors not addressed [in the critical reflection on terrorism, political violence, American foreign policy, and socio-economics] was religion."[22] Exploring the role of religion as a significant factor in response to "mass atrocities" is also

[18] Wellman, Jr., and Tokuno, "Is Religious Violence Inevitable?," p. 295; see also Appleby, *The Ambivalence of the Sacred*, pp. 1-3; Linda Woodhead, "Restoring Religion to the Public Square," in *The Tablet*, January 28, 2012, pp. 6-7.

[19] See Juergensmeyer, *Terror in the Mind of God*, p. 224.

[20] James K. Wellman, Jr., "Religion and Violence: Past, Present, and Future," in Wellman, Jr. (Ed.), *Belief and Bloodshed*, p. 1; see also Kee, *Constantine versus Christ*, p. 1.

[21] Hanson, *Religion and Politics in the International System Today*, p. 296.

[22] Tite, "Sacred Violence and the Scholar of Religion as Public Intellectual," in Rennie and Tite (Eds.), *Religion, Terror and Violence*, p. 4; see also p. 5.

important. In this regard, Thomas Brudholm and Thomas Cushman write that "religious discourses and practices have seeped into broader, public, and secular discourse and contexts."[23]

As I pointed out in the previous chapter, religion is also an essential player in the search for justice. As Eric O. Hanson states,

> Religion and politics thus constitute an integrating "united front" against the EMC [Economic, Military, and Communication] systems. In a mature civil society, religious and political leaders should not only serve as checks on each other, but together they should seek to defend the society from the EMC monopoly practices. The EMC systems must be limited by the political system in the first part of the paradigm and by religious experience in the second.[24]

He adds further on that, in the context of the important role of religion in the search for global justice, "[g]lobal equity is the primary political-religious issue for the next one hundred years."[25] For this reason, he concludes, the search for "global equity" is often linked to the search for "environmental justice."[26] The contribution of religion to peace and to a just, sustainable world order is underlined by Willard M. Swartly as well:

> In light of the contemporary urgent need to correlate peace with justice, Luke creatively and profoundly speaks to our needs as well as those in his time. The meaning of justice in both Deuteronomy and Luke is not to be confused with the Greek notion of rendering to every one his or her due, but must be understood in parallel to mercy as shown in God's covenant relationship to Israel. Seeing the needs of the poor and marginalized, it responds with compassion.[27]

[23] Brudholm and Cushman, "Introduction," in Brudholm and Cushman (Eds.), *The Religious in Responses to Mass Atrocity*, p. 2.

[24] Hanson, *Religion and Politics in the International System Today*, p. 45.

[25] Hanson, *Religion and Politics in the International System Today*, p. 61. Jamal Khader adds his voice as well to the link between religion and justice, recognizing that justice is the best guaranty for peace (see "Opportunities and Threats for Religions in Conflict and Violence," in Haers, Hintersteiner and Schrijver [Eds], *Postcolonial Europe in the Crucible of Cultures*, pp. 160-161).

[26] See Hanson, *Religion and Politics in the International System Today*, p. 61.

[27] Swartly, *Covenant of Peace*, p. 43. The relationship between justice and mercy is an essential dimension of the three monotheistic religions, and stressing this relationship has probably been one of their best contributions to peace and to processes of reconciliation. This is also highlighted in Pope John Paul II's second Encyclical *Dives in Misericordia* (*"Rich in Mercy"*), at http://www.vatican.va/holy_father/john_paul_ii/encyclicals/documents/hf_jp-ii_enc_30111980_dives-in-misericordia_en.html (accessed September 29, 2011). In this Encyclical, the Pope, without denying the importance of justice, refers to the fact that justice without mercy can be a hidden form of revenge. It is also within this context that "restorative justice" emerges, namely, a more humane way of assuring justice,

Especially when we take cognizence of the cultural and socio-political dimensions of religion and their relationship to the need to confront violence and promote justice, we can appreciate the fact that religion has an important role to play in processes of forgiveness and reconciliation. In a particular way, the religious conception of forgiveness is essential to these processes. As Redekop says,

> [f]orgiveness is giving up the right to retribution. It involves a conscious decision to block the emotional default setting that prompts us to mimic violence and desire harm for our adversary. Signals of forgiveness can indicate that, at a minimum, no further harm is intended although distance, both physical and spiritual, may be needed. At a maximum, it results in an enthusiastic, from-the-heart desire for the well-being and prosperity of the adversary. At a minimum, signals of forgiveness are a will and resolve to stop the escalating cycle of violence and revenge.[28]

In this regard, Thomas Brudholm and Thomas Cushman underline the greater visibility of religious actors in processes of societal healing. They write: "In countries like South Africa, Sierra Leone, and Northern Ireland, [and Canada,] religious leaders and organizations have been related to state-sponsored truth commissions and faith-based diplomacy, and ideals and practices of forgiveness, reconciliation and commemoration have become part of current political discourse and practice."[29] Along with other contributors in the volume from which this note is taken, they insist that forgiveness, as is the case with other religious concepts, cannot be used to justify violence or to give to violence any transcendent meaning.[30] That is why, in order to overcome a false understanding

by implicating offenders, victims of violence, and the community at large in the process of healing (see Howard Zehr, *El pequeño libro de la Justicia Restaurativa*, Intercouse: Good Books, 2007; Tutu with Abrams, *God Has a Dream*, pp. 8-11).

[28] Redekop, *From Violence to Blessing*, p. 298. Forgiveness is, as Alan Storkey, notes so well, the contrary of "self-vindication": "Self-vindication often goes with failure. It allows us to ignore our own faults and exaggerates those of the enemy. Scapegoating, another stage in the process, retains the enemy as the problem and can last for centuries, as it has in the Balkans. The human ability to identify enemies and become convinced that only the enemy is wrong is rampant" (*Jesus and Politics*, p. 157).

[29] Brudholm and Cushman, "Introduction," in Brudhom and Cushman (Eds.), *The Religious in Responses to Mass Atrocity*, pp. 3-4.

[30] See Brudholm and Cushman, "Introduction," in Brudhom and Cushman (Eds.), *The Religious in Responses to Mass Atrocity*, pp. 4-5; see also Geddes, "Religious Rhetoric in Response to Atrocity," in Brudholm and Cushman (Eds.), *The Religious in Responses to Mass Atrocity*, pp. 21, 27, 31-32. Thus, regarding the risk of a distorted utilization of religious concepts on believers, Brudholm says: "In relation to victims who are Christians, I wonder whether such statements or the invocation of Jesus on the cross and the attitude

of forgiveness, believers have to address it in relationship to forgetting and to reconciliation.[31]

Dealing with the importance of forgiveness in all dimensions of life, human and spiritual, Jean Monbourquette (1933–2011) underscores the fact that forgiveness is neither forgetting nor denial; it is not the result of willpower; it cannot be given on command, or signify a return to the past before the offense. It does not mean giving up victims' rights, excusing the offender, demonstrating moral superiority, or leaving it up to God.[32] Even when recognizing the right to defend and protect oneself against violence, it is important to avoid retaliation, and to decide not to respond to violence with further violence. Reacting violently can be an instinctive response on the part of the offended person. Yet, by reacting in this way, the person merely perpetuates the cycle of violence and risks, in turn, becoming an offender. At stake is that person's own integrity and dignity.[33]

Forgiveness does not necessarily imply reconciliation with the offender, even if, ideally, reconciliation can be considered the summit of forgiveness, the manifestation of a new beginning.[34] Forgiveness means that the person no longer harbors any desire for revenge. In no longer doing so, forgiveness produces a sense of liberation from an internal burden: "Advocates typically stress that forgiving benefits and liberates forgivers from the past and keeps them from wallowing in resentment and fantasies of revenge. Indeed, the overcoming or letting go of these often unpleasant repercussions of injury are central in most attempts to define or account for the nature of forgiveness."[35] When the offended

of God to his creation put improper pressure on the believer to comply with what is at least partially also a political agenda" (Thomas Brudholm, "On the Advocacy of Forgiveness after Mass Atrocity," in Brudholm and Cushman [Eds.], *The Religious in Responses to Mass Atrocity*, p. 143). A few pages later, speaking of forgiveness in particular, Brudholm concludes saying: "I have argued that, indeed, the advocacy of forgiveness can become a liability to the victims, and it is important to be alert to this when forgiveness is mobilized as the key to peace, reconciliation, or the transformation of hearts and minds" (p. 146; see also Martínez de Pisón, "Enrichie par la guérison," pp. 23-25).

[31] See Martínez de Pisón, "Enrichie par la guérison," pp. 19-21.

[32] See Jean Monbourquette, *How to Forgive: A Step-by-Step Guide* (K. Poor and G. Gasslein, trans.), Ottawa: Novalis, 2007 (©2000), pp. 31-43.

[33] See Monbourquette, *How to Forgive*, pp. 24-25.

[34] Mobourquette, in the last step of his twelve-step guide to forgiveness, takes as his starting point that forgiveness is not synonymous with reconciliation. This idea is very useful in indicating to victims when and if they should decide to end or to renew the relationship with the perpetrator of violence (see *How to Forgive*, pp. 179-190).

[35] Brudholm, "On the Advocacy of Forgiveness after Mass Atrocity," in Brudholm and Cushman (Eds.), *The Religious in Responses to Mass Atrocity*, p. 125.

person is thus freed, he or she may be able to say to the perpetrator of violence: "I forgive you, but I am no longer willing to accept how you treated me."

However, it is not always possible, for different reasons, to be reconciled to the one who acts violently. Whereas the act of forgiving implicates the offended person only, independently of the process in which the offender is involved, reconciliation supposes that two persons or groups are in the same process of healing and would require that the perpetrator of violence be repentant.[36] Sometimes reconciliation is not desired by the offended person, even if he or she has forgiven the offender. The victim may have lost trust in the perpetrator, or simply be afraid of reassuming the relationship. It may even be that in a given situation reconciliation may not be recommended. This may be the case particularly when, for example, the offender is dangerous or the one responsible for the violence does not show signs of remorse.

Even with these somewhat qualifying remarks in mind concerning religion's role in relation to reconciliation, we can surely conclude that religion as such is a mobilizing force. If in the past religion was often utilized to justify violence, today's challenge for religion consists in its becoming a partner, along with many other socio-political and economic players, in the search for justice and peace. For these reasons, Madawi Al-Rasheed and Marat Shterin assert: "[T]he public sphere must show flexibility in accepting and recognizing that there is ample space for religious groups to contribute to public life and policy; exclusion will never serve as an incentive for moderation."[37] Religion, then, should be better integrated into public life in today's world.

* * *

The sixth and final conclusion to be drawn is the need to reintegrate religion into public life. As Mark Juergensmeyer says:

[36] See Nigel Biggar, "The Ethics of Forgiveness and the Doctrine of Just War: A Religious View of Righting Atrocious Wrongs," in Brudholm and Cushman (Eds.), *The Religious in Responses to Mass Atrocity*, pp. 110-111.

[37] Madawi Al-Rasheed and Marat Shterin, "Introduction: Between Death of Faith and Dying for Faith: Reflections on Religion, Politics, Society and Violence," in Madawi Al-Rasheed and Marat Shterin (Eds.), *Dying for Faith: Religiously Motivated Violence in the Contemporary World*, London (UK), New York: I. B. Tauris & Co. Ltd., 2009, p. xxix.

> Religion gives spirit to public life and provides a beacon for moral order. At the same time it needs the temper of rationality and fair play that Enlightenment values give to civil society. Thus religious violence cannot end until some accommodation can be forged between the two–some assertion of moderation in religion's passion, and some acknowledgement of religion in elevating the spiritual and moral values of public life. In a curious way, then, the cure for religious violence may ultimately lie in a renewed appreciation for religion itself.[38]

Religion is one indispensable player and a particularly important partner in the search for meaning, justice, peace, forgiveness and reconciliation.[39] It contributes by bringing a consideration of profound values to society and to discussion in the public sphere. As Oliver J. McTerman notes, "[a] common complaint of the religious terrorists, whatever their faith tradition, is the absence of values in a world that has excluded God. Their common goal is to make religion the 'foundation' of a new social order."[40] Yet, the terrorist's view of religion as "the 'foundation' of a new social order" brings us closer to an apocalyptic scenario than to peace. For this reason, religious leaders, above all those within Judaism, Christianity, and Islam, must contribute to presenting their common faith in the God of the Covenant as faith in a God who announces a new creation where justice and peace will be a reality for all people and all nations. This is a God totally opposed to any kind of intentionally provoked violence and, especially, to the religious justification of such violence.

[38] Juergensmeyer, *Terror in the Mind of God*, p. 243.

[39] See Clayton Crockett, "Introduction," in Crockett (Ed.), *Religion and Violence in a Secular World*, pp. 10-11, 17-18.

[40] McTerman, *Violence in God's Name*, p. xvii.

Summary and Conclusions

In this book, I have progressively drawn a series of six conclusions. The first of these conclusions referred to the fact that religion is not, intrinsically speaking, a source of violence. Any religious justification of violence is the result of the unfair manipulation of religion for violent purposes. In such manipulation, the Divine becomes domesticated, a God made in our own "image" and "likeness." When religion is used to justify violence, it no longer functions as a means for entering into relationship with the transcendent Other. It becomes, rather, an ideology. The liturgical worship of the Divine is then transformed into idolatry: we worship a false god. In contrast, I have suggested that peace is the essence of religion and true worship of God always involves fostering peace.

The second conclusion is the need to put an end to "the myth of redemptive violence," and to the wrongful use of God's name to justify violence. This applies to counter-violence and its supposedly, but deeply questioned, moral justification. The mistreatment of God's name within Judaism, Christianity, and Islam, by using it to justify violence is one of the most terrible abuses of religion. To overcome such religious justification of violence means liberating God from the "prison" into which we have enclosed the Divine. We have perverted God's name in the past, and we continue to do so now every time we use God's name to legitimize the dehumanization of others.

The third conclusion drawn is the importance of taking into account the victims of violence, particularly the most vulnerable, who can easily be forgotten. In this regard, religious leaders and believers in general need to develop a pastoral care of compassion in order to be attentive to the suffering inflicted upon children, adolescents, aboriginal peoples, the LGBTQ community, and women in general. Furthermore, we pointed out how, contrary to the image of a "warrior" and almost "pathological" God, God is primarily the God of the victim. Religious violence inflicted upon anyone, but especially on the most vulnerable in society, is a betrayal of God's name.

The fourth conclusion is that perpetrators of violence are also its victims. Often, they have themselves previously been victims of violence and they, now in turn, perpetrate violence, becoming themselves victims as well of their own violent behavior. This implies the recognition of their own humanity. Rather than demonizing and scapegoating them, we should be able to look at them with God's eyes and recognize that they too reveal to us important dimensions of ourselves. In addition, and in relationship to my main thesis on the link between religion and violence, I emphasized the need to pay attention to shame, especially in its negative relation to violence. Without being able to heal toxic, unhealthy shame in its personal and social dimensions, we will find it very difficult trying to break out of the spiral of violence.

The fifth conclusion is the conviction that true religion is incompatible with provoked violence. This is why peace and its establishment can be considered the most important criterion for discerning the "authenticity" of a religion, and the "veracity" of its Holy Scriptures. Furthermore, in relation to establishing peace I have addressed the need of overcoming patriarchy, as one of the ideological infrastructures that has sustained the inequalities between men and women and facilitated the destruction of the environment. Thus, religion should promote gender equality and a more respectful partnership between human beings and the environment as a way of nurturing peace.

The sixth, and last, conclusion concerned the necessity of fostering a re-integration of religion into public life, while taking their respective boundaries into account. In order to do so, we must overcome the idolization of privacy. The taboo of privacy and the confusion between the private and the personal affect in a negative and limiting way the understanding of religion which should be seen as representing a personal dimension of a human being who is open to others, to creation, and to God, that is to say, a person who is a social and political being. Religion, therefore, plays an important role in both personal life and in society. This is why the recognition of the cultural, socio-political, economical and environmental dimensions of religion are crucial in the process of building up a culture of justice, equality, and peace.

Finally, I would like to point out three aspects which I consider essential to the present endeavor to overcome the detrimental link that exists between religion and violence when religion is used to justify or excuse violence. The first aspect refers to the importance of keeping justice and mercy together. Without mercy, we are not able to exit from the spiral of violence. We continue demonizing others and, in the end, we destroy our own dignity. To look at the other with God's eyes signifies recognizing in the other, even in the enemy, God's own "image" and "likeness."

The second aspect deals with the necessity of entering into the difficult, but necessary, process of remembering the past if we wish to establish the truth of what really happened in a given situation. This is the only way for us to arrive at forgiveness and reconciliation. Forgiveness is not synonymous with forgetting.

The third and final aspect concerns the responsibility that religious leaders have, particularly within the three monotheistic faiths, to address believers in catechetical and pastoral milieus on the incongruity of using God's name for any justification of provoked violence. To do this, religious leaders are morally obliged to deal with thc question of God being considered as "the true author" of the Holy Scriptures. It would be impossible to overcome the problem of toxic scriptural texts without at least questioning the "divine inspiration" of these "dark" texts, to use the expression of Pope Benedict XVI. Therefore, Jews, Christians, and Muslims have to own God's commandment: "You shall not make wrongful use of the name of the LORD your God, for the LORD will not acquit anyone who misuses his name" (Ex 20:7). Texts, even toxic sacred texts, do not kill by themselves; only people do. We have to end the projections of our own morbid tendencies on to the Divine.

Selected Bibliography

Academy of Humanism, *Neo-Fundamentalism: The Humanist Response*, Buffalo: Prometheus Books, 1988.

Al-Rasheed, Madawi and Shterin, Marat (Eds.), *Dying for Faith: Religiously Motivated Violence in the Contemporary World*, London (UK) and New York: I. B. Tauris & Co. Ltd., 2009.

Appleby, R. Scott, *The Ambivalence of the Sacred: Religion, Violence, and Reconciliation*, Lanham: Rowman & Littlefield Publishers, Inc. (Carnegie Commission on Preventing Deadly Conflict Series), 2000.

Armistead, M. Kathryn, *God-Images in the Healing Process*, Minneapolis: Fortress Press, 1995.

Assmann, Jan, *Religion and Cultural Memory: Ten Studies*, Stanford: Stanford University Press (Cultural Memory in the Present), 2006.

Bellet, Maurice, *Le Dieu pervers* (Nouvelle édition), Paris: Desclée de Brower, 2002 (©1998).

Bellet, Maurice, *"Je ne suis pas venu apporter la paix…": Essai sur la violence absolue*, Paris: Éditions Albin Michel, 2009.

Bellinger, Charles K., *The Genealogy of Violence: Reflections on Creation, Freedom, and Evil*, Oxford (UK): Oxford University Press, 2001.

Bennett, Clinton, *In Search of Solutions: The Problem of Religion and Conflict*, London (UK), Oakville: Equinox Publishing Ltd. (Religion and Violence), 2008.

Boff, Leonardo, *Trinité et société* (F. Malley, trans.), Paris: Éditions du Cerf (Libération, 5), 1990.

Boff, Leonardo, *Cry of the Earth, Cry of the Poor* (Ph. Berryman, trans.), Maryknowll: Orbis Books, 2005 (©1997).

Bradshaw, John, *Healing the Shame that Binds You*, Deerfield Beach: Health Communications, Inc., 1988.

Bregman, Lucy, *Beyond Silence and Denial: Death and Dying Reconsidered*, Louisville: Westminster John Knox Press, 1999.

Bregman, Lucy, *Death and Dying, Spirituality and Religions: A Study of the Death Awareness Movement*, New York: Peter Lang Publishing, Inc. (American University Studies. Series VII: Theology and Religion, 228), 2003.

Brudholm, Thomas and Cushman, Thomas (Eds.), *The Religious in Responses to Mass Atrocity: Interdisciplinary Perspectives*, New York: Cambridge University Press, 2009.

Capps, Donal, *The Depleted Self: Sin in a Narcissistic Age*, Minneapolis: Fortress Press, 1993.

Causse, Jean Daniel, Cuvillier, Élian and Wénin, André, *Divine violence: Approche exégétique et anthropologique*, Paris: Éditions du Cerf, Médiaspaul (Lire la Bible, 168), 2011.

Chance, Sue, *Stronger than Death*, New York, London (UK): W. W. Norton & Company, 1992.

Coriden, James A. (Ed.), *Sexim and Church Law: Equal Rights and Affirmative Action*, New York: Paulist Press, 1977.

Cote, Richard G., *Re-Visioning Mission: The Catholic Church and Culture in Postmodern America*, New York, Mahwah: Paulist Press, 1996.

Crockett, Clayton (Ed.), *Religion and Violence in a Secular World: Toward a New Political Theology*, Charlottesville, London (UK): University of Virginia Press (Studies in Religion and Culture), 2006.

Dumais, Monique, *Femmes et mondialisation*, Montréal: Médiaspaul (Interpellations), 2009.

Dupré, Louis, *The Other Dimension: A Search for the Meaning of Religious Attitudes*, Garden City: Doubleday, 1972.

Ellens, J. Harold (Ed.), *The Destructive Power of Religion: Violence in Judaism, Christianity, and Islam*, vol. 1 (Sacred Scriptures, Ideology, and Violence), Westport, Connecticut, London (UK): Praeger (Contemporary Psychology), 2004.

Ellens, J. Harold (Ed.), *The Destructive Power of Religion: Violence in Judaism, Christianity, and Islam*, vol. 2 (Religion, Psychology, and Violence), Westport, Connecticut, London (UK): Praeger (Contemporary Psychology), 2004.

Ellens, J. Harold (Ed.), *The Destructive Power of Religion: Violence in Judaism, Christianity, and Islam*, vol. 3 (Models and Cases of Violence in Religion), Westport, Connecticut, London (UK): Praeger (Contemporary Psychology), 2004.

Ellens, J. Harold (Ed.), *The Destructive Power of Religion: Violence in Judaism, Christianity, and Islam*, vol. 4 (Contemporary Views on Spirituality and Violence), Westport, Connecticut, London (UK): Praeger (Contemporary Psychology), 2004.

Ellul, Jacques, *Violence: Reflections from a Christian Perspective* (C. G. Kings, trans.), New York: Seabury Press, 1969.

Fowler, James W., *Stages of Faith: The Psychology of Human Development and the Quest for Meaning*, New York: Harper & Row, 1981.

Gilligan, James, *Violence: Reflections on a National Epidemic*, New York: Vintage Books, 1996.

Girard, René, *Je vois Satan tomber comme l'éclair*, Paris: Bernard Grasset, 1999.

Goldberg, Carl, *Understanding Shame*, Northvale, London (UK): Jason Aronson Inc., 1991.

Gopin, Marc, *Between Eden and Armageddon: The Future of World Religions, Violence and Peacemaking*, Oxford (UK), Toronto: Oxford University Press, 2000.

Griffith, Lee, *The War on Terrorism and the Terror of God*, Grand Rapids, Cambridge (UK): William B. Eerdmans Publishing Co., 2002.

Haers, Jacques, Hintersteiner, Norbert and Schrijver, Georges De (Eds.), *Postcolonial Europe in the Crucible of Cultures: Reckoning with God in a World of Conflicts*, Amsterdam, New York: Rodopi (Currents of Encounter, 34), 2007.

Hanson, Eric O., *Religion and Politics in the International System Today*, New York: Cambridge University Press, 2006.

Hedges, Chris, *War Is a Force that Gives Us Meaning*, New York: Anchor Books, 2003 (©2002).

Hendricks, Obery M., Jr., *The Politics of Jesus: Rediscovering the True Revolutionary Nature of the Teaching of Jesus and How They Have Been Corrupted*, New York: Doubleday, 2006.

Hommer-Dixon, Thomas F., *Environment, Scarcity, and Violence*, Princeton: Princeton University Press, 1999.

Isherwood, Lisa and Ruether, Rosemary Radford (Eds.), *Weep Not for Your Children: Essays on Religion and Violence*, London (UK), Oakville: Equinox Publishing Ltd., 2008.

Jones, James W., *In the Middle of this Road We Call Our Life: The Courage to Search for Something More*, San Francisco: HarperSanFrancisco (Psychology/Spirituality), 1995.

Juergensmeyer, Mark, *Terror in the Mind of God: The Global Rise of Religious Violence* (Updated edition with a new preface), Berkeley, Los Angeles, London (UK): University of California Press (Comparative Studies in Religion and Society, 13), 2001 (©2000).

Kasper, Walter, *The God of Jesus Christ* (M. J. O'Connell, trans.), New York: Crossroad, 1984.

Kee, Alistair, *Constantine versus Christ: The Triumph of Ideology*, London (UK): SCM Press Ltd., 1982.

Küng, Hans, *Islam: Past, Present and Future* (J. Bowden, trans.), Oxford (UK): Oneworld Publications (The Religious Situation of our Time, [3]), 2007.

Lawrence, Bruce B., *Defender of God: The Fundamentalist Revolt against the Modern Age*, San Francisco: Harper & Row, 1989.

Lévi-Strauss, Claude, *Tristes tropiques*, Paris: Plon (Terre Humaine), 1955.

Lévi-Strauss, Claude, *Anthropologie structurale*, Paris: Plon, 1958.

Lévi-Strauss, Claude, *La pensée sauvage*, Paris: Plon, 1963.

Lévi-Strauss, Claude, *L'origine des manières de table*, Paris: Plon (Mythologiques, 3), 1968.

Lewis, Hellen B. (Ed.), *The Role of Shame in Symptom Formation*, Hillsdale, London (UK): Laurence Erlbaum Associates, 1987.

Lewis, Michael, *Shame: The Exposed Self*, New York: The Free Press, 1992.

Marguerat, Daniel (Ed.), *Dieu est-il violent?*, Paris: Bayard Édition, 2008.

Martínez de Pisón, Ramón, *Sin and Evil* (R. R. Cooper, trans.), Sherbrooke: Médiaspaul, 2002.

Martínez de Pisón, Ramón, *Death by Despair: Shame and Suicide*, New York: Peter Lang Publishing, Inc. (American University Studies. Series VII: Theology and Religion, 245), 2006.

Martínez de Pisón, Ramón, *Life beyond Death: The Eschatological Dimension of Christian Faith*, Ottawa: Novalis, 2007.

Martínez de Pisón, Ramón, *Dieu est unique mais non solitaire: Vie trinitaire et transformation humaine*, Montréal, Médiaspaul (Brèches Théologiques, 43), 2008.

Martínez de Pisón, Ramón, *God: From Knowing to Experiencing*, Toronto: Novalis Publishing Inc., 2009.

Marx, Karl, *Economic and Philosophic Manuscripts of 1844* (M. Milligan, trans.), Moscow: Foreign Languages Publication House, 1961.

McFague, Sallie, *The Body of God: An Ecological Theology*, Minneapolis: Fortress Press, 1993.

McTernan, Oliver J., *Violence in God's Name: Religion in an Age of Conflict*, Maryknoll: Orbis Books, 2003.

Meslin, Michel, *L'expérience humaine du divin: Fondements d'une anthropologie religieuse*, Paris: Éditions du Cerf (Cogitatio Fidei, 150), 1988.

Monbourquette, Jean, *How to Forgive: A Step-by-Step Guide* (K. Poor and G. Gasslein, trans.), Ottawa: Novalis, 2007 (©2000).

Mooren, Thomas, *War and Peace in Monotheistic Religions*, Delhi: Media House, 2008.

Nason-Clark, Nancy, *The Battered Wife: How Christians Confront Family Violence*, Louisville: Westminster John Knox Press, 1997.

Nathanson, Donald L., *Shame and Pride: Affect, Sex, and the Birth of the Self*, New York, London (UK): W. W. Norton & Company, Inc., 1992.

Nelson-Pallmeyer, Jack, *Jesus against Christianity: Reclaiming the Missing Jesus*, Harrisburg, Pennsylvania: Trinity Press International, 2001.

Nelson-Pallmeyer, Jack, *Is Religion Killing Us?: Violence in the Bible and the Quran*, Harrisburg, London (UK), New York: Trinity Press International, 2003.

Noël, Pierre (Ed.), *Mondialisation, violence et religion*, Montréal: Fides (Hétirage et Projet, 74), 2009.

Northcott, Michael, *An Angel Directs the Storm: Apocalyptic Religion and American Empire*, London (UK): SCM Press, 2007.

Nouwen, Henri J. M., *Reaching Out: The Three Movements of the Spiritual Life*, Garden City: Doubleday & Company Inc., 1975.

O'Faolain, Julia, and Martines, Lauro (Eds.), *Not in God's Image: Women in History from the Greeks to the Victorians*, New York, Evanston, San Francisco, London (UK): Harper & Row (Harper Torchbook), 1973.

Onfray, Michel, *Traité d'athéologie: Physique de la métaphysique*, Paris: Bernard Grasset, 2005.

Pattison, Stephen, *Shame: Theory, Therapy, Theology*, Cambridge (UK): Cambridge University Press, 2000.

Perrin, David B., *Studying Christian Spirituality*, New York, London (UK): Routledge (Religion and Spirituality), 2007.

Peterson, V. Spike and Runyan, Anne Sisson, *Global Gender Issues*, Boulder, San Francisco, Oxford (UK): Westview Press (Dilemmas in World Politics), 1993.

Primavesi, Anne, *Gaia's Gift: Earth, Ourselves and God after Copernicus*, London (UK), New York: Routledge, 2003.

Rapley, Elizabeth, *The Lord as Their Portion: The Story of the Religious Orders and How They Shaped Our World*, Grand Rapids, Toronto: William B. Eerdmans Publishing Co., Novalis, 2011.

Ratzinger, Joseph [Pope Benedict XVI], *Eschatology: Death and Eternal Life* (M. Waldestein, trans.), Washington: Catholic University of America Press (Dogmatic Theology, 9), 1988.

Redekop, Vernon Neufeld, *Scapegoats, the Bible, and Criminal Justice: Interacting with René Girard*, Akron: Mennonite Central Committee (Issue no. 13), 1993.

Redekop, Vernon Neufeld, *From Violence to Blessing: How an Understanding of Deep-Rooted Conflict Can Open Paths to Reconciliation*, Ottawa: Novalis, 2002.

Rennie, Bryan and Tite, Philip L. (Eds.), *Religion, Terror and Violence: Religious Studies Perspectives*, New York, London (UK): Routledge, 2008.

Ress, Mary Judith, *Ecofeminism in Latin America*, Maryknoll: Orbis Books (Women from the Margins), 2006.

Rizzuto, Ana María, *The Birth of the Living God: A Psychoanalytic Study*, Chicago: The University of Chicago Press, 1979.

Ruether, Rosemery Radford, *Gaia and God: An Ecofeminist Theology of Earth Healing*, San Francisco: HarperSanFrancisco, 1992.

Scherper-Hughes, Nancy and Bourgois, Philippe (Eds.), *Violence in War and Peace; An Anthology*, Malden: Blackwell Publishing, 2004.

Schüssler Fiorenza, Elisabeth, *In Memory of Her: A Feminist Theological Reconstruction of Christian Origins* (Tenth Anniversary Edition: With a New Introduction), New York: Crossroad, 1994 (©1983).

Schüssler Fiorenza, Elisabeth (Ed.), *The Power of Naming: A Concilium Reader in Feminist Liberation Theology*, Maryknoll, London (UK): Orbis Books, SCM Press (Concilium Series), 1996.

Schwarz, Hans, *Eschatology*, Grand Rapids: William B. Eerdmans Publishing Co., 2000.

Stassen, Glen Harold and Gushee, David P., *Kingdom Ethics: Following Jesus in Contemporary Context*, Downers Grove: InterVarsity Press, 2003.

Stier, Oren Baruch and Landres, J. Shawn (Eds.), *Religion, Violence, Memory, and Place*, Bloomington: Indiana University Press, 2006.

Storkey, Alan, *Jesus and Politics: Confronting the Powers*, Grand Rapids: Baker Academic, 2005.

Swartly, Willard M., *Covenant of Peace: The Missing Peace in New Testament Theology and Ethics*, Grand Rapids, Cambridge (UK): William B. Eerdmans Publishing Co., 2006.

Tribble, Philys, *Texts of Terror: Literary-Feminist Readings of Biblical Narratives*, Philadelphia: Fortress Press (Overtures to Biblical Theology, 13), 1984.

Vickers, Jeanne, *Women and War*, London (UK), New Jersey: Zed Books, 1993.

Watson, John, *The Interpretation of Religious Experience* (The Gifford Lectures, 1910–1912), vol. 1 (Historical), New York: AMS Press, 1979 (©1912).

Wellman, James K., Jr. (Ed.), *Belief and Bloodshed: Religion and Violence across Time and Tradition*, Lanham: Rowman & Littlefield Publishers, Inc., 2007.

Wenham, David, *Paul: Follower of Jesus or Founder of Christianity?*, Grand Rapids, Cambridge (UK): William B. Eerdmans Publishing Co., 1995.

Wiley, Tatha, *Original Sin: Origins, Developments, Contemporary Meanings*, New York: Paulist Press, 2002.

Wink, Walter, *Engaging the Powers: Discernment and Resistance in a World of Domination*, Minneapolis: Fortress Press, 1992.
Wink, Walter, *The Powers That Be: Theology for a New Millennium*, New York: Galilee Doubleday, 1998.
Zehr, Howard, *El pequeño libro de la Justicia Restaurativa*, Intercouse: Good Books, 2007.

Index

PRINTED ON PERMANENT PAPER • IMPRIME SUR PAPIER PERMANENT • GEDRUKT OP DUURZAAM PAPIER - ISO 9706

N.V. PEETERS S.A., WAROTSTRAAT 50, B-3020 HERENT